OVERCOMING ALL ODDS: TWO

The College Years: Challenges Met

Ron N. Reel Ph.D.

FOREWORD

This book continues the story of my life, begun in my first memoir, *Overcoming All Odds*, published in 2019. That volume chronicled my life from birth through high school graduation and the death of my mother, to my enrollment at Bethany Bible College. With God's help, I survived a number of serious illnesses, extreme poverty, and the mental and physical abuse of my father. In this installment I relate events from the summer of 1968 through the summer of 1974, discussing the four colleges I attended and noting the unique challenges each of them provided. I had to overcome academic and personal challenges, including accusations of plagiarism, negative stereotyping, too much alcohol consumption, and my own lack of self-confidence, all of which resulted in a bout of acute depression. I describe the various jobs I undertook to pay for my college education. Once again, God sent teachers and friends to help me overcome all obstacles and to keep my college education on track. I hope that my story will encourage you to take on and defeat your own demons and to help others overcome theirs.

To recall these events, I had to depend primarily on my own memory. Of course, I also consulted with some of the people with whom I shared this journey to answer any questions I had about the events I discussed.

In fact, some of these events were painful to revisit and I had suppressed them for many years.

I did much soul searching and many rewrites to capture each event so that my depiction of them would be honest and accurate. Certainly, my college experience was a rollercoaster ride that I was not prepared to take by myself; and again, had it not been for several teachers who showed me great kindness, provided me needed direction, and gave me the tools to gain self-respect I would not have overcome the obstacles I encountered during this time and been able to achieve my bachelor's and master's degrees.

My perceptions are my reality and others may remember differently the same situations I describe here. My biological father returned for a portion of these years and his reappearance continued his negative impact on my life. I did not change his name, but I have renamed a few other participants to avoid any embarrassment they might experience from the publication of this manuscript. No one should assume to be a particular individual unless I have identified them by his or her legal name. Occasionally, I combined the actions of two or more people into the actions of one.

I want to thank Carolyn Inmon and John Arrijuria for proofreading my manuscript. I wish also to acknowledge the help of Dr. Hal Bochin, a long-time mentor, who has served as my chief editor, strong enough to advise me when too much had been said in a particular chapter and able to point out when more needed to be shared in another. Any remaining errors are mine alone.

CHAPTER ONE

I got up early on Friday morning anticipating what it would be like to leave the Bakersfield area and to move all the way to Scotts Valley, which is six miles north of Santa Cruz. I had not slept much. My mind kept returning to the week before, which had been the most difficult week of my life. My mother had passed away; my father had caused a fight with other family members, resulting in my two younger sisters having to live with older siblings; and I found him with another woman living at his home. I was homeless. Today was going to be the first day of what was going to be a journey that would change my life forever.

The Waldrip family had become important to me because, from time to time, they had allowed me to stay at their home a night or two when things had gotten too chaotic at my house. Jim and Leta Mae had two children: Marilyn, who was two years older than I, and Gerald, who was two years younger than I. Jim had been my barber from the time I was twelve when I lived in Wasco and Shafter. Leta Mae always made sure that I had enough to eat.

Marilyn had been attending Bakersfield Junior College for the past two years and had just graduated with a 4.0 grade point average. She had chosen a business and accounting major. She was known for her intellect, hard work, and perseverance. Marilyn had shoulder length dark black hair, dark eyes, and a great smile. She sang in the church choir and taught children's Bible school. Marilyn did not date often. Her parents were always kidding her about the lack of dating in her life. Her father once told her, "We want you to go to Bethany or some other Bible college and come out with an MRS Degree." After two years at Bakersfield College, she had applied to several four-year colleges and decided to transfer to Bethany as a junior. Since we were both going to be attending Bethany at the same time, she offered me the opportunity to ride to the college with her. I arrived at their house at 7:00 a.m. as instructed.

Pastor Gould had been kind enough to take me to the Waldrips' home. While we were driving there, he said, "This is going to be the start of what will change your life for the better; and because of that change will benefit your family members, your friends, and down the line, many people you have not yet met."

I listened but did not know how to respond. Finally, I told him, "This day would not have been possible had it not been for you, your family, your support, and your love for me. I will always appreciate it and give you special recognition should anything positive happen to me that results in changing other people's lives for the better."

He smiled and replied, "You have always been important to me. That first night I saw in you a quality that God has something special planned for you. It won't be easy, but you, with His help, will figure it out. If you need me, I will be just a phone call away."

We pulled up to the Waldrip family home and found they were all outside. They had given Marilyn a new Chevy Malibu two years earlier for college transportation. The trunk was open, and I could see it was full of personal items she was taking with her. They turned around and started waving to Pastor and me. I knew that they were grateful that Pastor had brought me. It was also an opportunity for Pastor to say goodbye to Marilyn.

Mrs. Waldrip spoke first, "Ron, we are really glad you are going to drive with Marilyn. It is nice knowing she will have a male traveling with her as we let our little girl go that far away from us. Do you have your things with you? There is not much room left. We can always send them by mail if you two need more room." I wanted to assure her that it would not take much room for my things as I answered. "I only have a few bags with me. I am sure I can place them in the trunk or in the back-seat area."

Mr. Waldrip wanted us to get on the road quickly to ensure we had plenty of time to arrive at Bethany and get checked into the dorms before dark. He looked at Pastor Gould, "Will you pray for their safety, Pastor?" he asked.

Pastor had us get in a circle and hold hands, "Heavenly Father, have your hand of protection over Marilyn and Ron as they travel from this location to Bethany Bible College. May you not only protect them today, but have your hand of love, compassion, understanding, and caring over them from this point forward. Make them ambassadors for your name and let those they encounter know your love through their actions, deeds, and person. Amen," he prayed.

I thought this might be the last time I would see Mr. and Mrs. Waldrip, who had been so kind to me. I would miss them. Marilyn and I got into the car. She started the engine and placed the car in reverse. We backed out of their driveway and I could hear their goodbyes as we started our journey.

I don't have any memory of the trip until we were passing the Denny's on Hwy 101 in Santa Cruz. I noticed a sign that directed us to Scotts Valley, seven miles ahead. I was very grateful for the ride; but knew my life at Bethany would be much more difficult than Marilyn's. She had a strong and caring family. Her parents and other relatives were financially stable and if she got into a pinch, needing financial assistance, help would be available. I knew my fate was in my own hands; but I knew that God would provide people to help me when I needed it most.

When we got to the college turn-off, I noticed on the right side of the freeway a sign for "Santa's Village." It was painted in a very Christmas spirit. There were cut-out figures of Santa, his helpers, candy canes, and artificial snow.

As we made our way under the freeway and turned onto the other side of the freeway, we started to travel up Bethany Drive, which had beautiful homes on both sides of the street, set back into the trees. It was breathtaking. I had never seen such a village of homes, all with nicely manicured lawns in a forest setting.

As we climbed higher, we could see the Bethany campus. The gym was on our right side. Just past the gym on the left was the chapel. In front of the chapel was a water fountain that had what looked like a globe of the world as a center piece with water rising from the middle cascading down and emptying into the base. We saw a dormitory just past the fountain, and in front of the dorm was a building that looked like it was home to several offices. As we approached, I read the words, "Admissions Office" on a glass door. On the right side of the street was the "Student Cafeteria." Marilyn kept driving. On the other side was a two-story building that had a sign reading, "Professor Offices and

Classrooms." As we drove higher, there was another dormitory on the left and another two-story building on the right that identified it as the "Student Store." We drove up past the second dorm. The sign designated it as the men's dorm. There was a road that looked like it made a loop around this building and came back down on the other side. It too had houses on both sides. They were not as nice as the ones we saw when we entered the college. Later I found out that these houses provided non-dormitory living for upper classmen.

Marilyn drove us back down the hill and we parked in front of the Admissions Office and we both entered. Quickly we were instructed that females and males were to register in opposite sides of the building. I told Marilyn that I would meet her outside near the car once I finished registering. I walked to the right side of the room through a glass door and was met by a smiling secretary who introduced herself as Barbara. She had a clipboard which held the names of all the newly enrolled male students.

I told her my name and she smiled again and said, "It is a pleasure to meet you. I see here you still need to complete some paperwork, take the Bible test, and then I can issue your dormitory keys and map of the campus." I thought I would need some additional paperwork because of the special favor that Pastor Kerns had made on my behalf.

I had no idea what the Bible test was all about, so I asked, "I am here and willing to take and do whatever is required so I can get settled. I did not know about a Bible test. What am I supposed to know?"

"It is the test all transfer and incoming students take so we can place them into the appropriate Bible courses based on their knowledge and understanding of the teachings found in the Bible," she said. I felt good about how that test would turn-out for me. I had memorized many scriptural passages and had even taught Sunday school classes occasionally.

"Where and when do I take the test?"

"If you are willing to do it now, I can have it administered right away," she replied.

"I am ready,"

"I am going to send you across the street over to the Student Cafeteria. One of our staff people will be in the back of the room. She can administer the test and then grade it on the spot. When you have it completed, return here and we can proceed," she instructed. I left the Administrative Office and went across the street to demonstrate my command and understanding of the Bible. As I entered the cafeteria, there was only one person at the back of the room. She waved for me to join her.

"I am Mrs. Hensley. Are you here to take your Bible test?" she asked.

"I am," I replied confidently.

"You need to complete it here so I can proctor the test. The test is 100 multiple choice questions. I will give you the test and an answer sheet. Make sure you completely fill the circle for each answer with your pencil because we use a key that sits over that test when we grade it. We mark with a red pen a completed circle for any questions that are wrong. You must earn 75% to skip the Bible Survey course. Do you have a pencil?" she asked.

"Yes. I am ready," I said as I took the test and answer sheet from her. I moved to a near-by table, pulled out the chair, and began reading the test questions. I began answering the questions without much concern. Most of the questions were simple and straightforward about various books, the people, and the activities that took place. When I completed the last question, I felt I had done well; at worse, I would miss one or two questions. It only took about fifteen minutes. I stood up and moved toward Mrs. Hensley.

"You have finished quickly. Do you want to go back over the test to see if you have made any errors?" she asked.

"No. I am confident. I am going to go outside and enjoy the fresh air and beautiful trees while you grade my test, if that is acceptable to you," I said. I did not want to brag about how well I had done until after she corrected my test. I went outside and took in the beauty of the setting. It was the prettiest place I had ever seen. I noticed that the only way to get to the gym was to walk over a man-made bridge. I could hear the babbling water running beneath the walking path as I crossed it. After a short while, I felt I had waited enough time for my test to be graded. I was sure there would only be one or two, if any, red marks on it; so, I returned to the cafeteria.

"Have you had time to correct my test?" Mrs. Hensley looked at me. She did not have what I thought was going to be a smile of astonishment over how well I had performed.

"You did not do well at all. You failed. In fact, it is one of the lowest scores I have ever seen," she said without a smile. I thought she was messing with me and waited for the smile.

"What do you mean? I think I may have gotten all of the questions right," I protested. I knew my answers were correct; well, almost all. I may have guessed at two; but through a process of elimination I was confident I had chosen the correct answer for at least one of them.

"See for yourself," she said as she handed me my scoresheet. It was full of red ink marks. I was very confused.

"This is not possible. Read me the questions. I know those answers,"
I pleaded.

"The test speaks for itself. Many students feel they know more than
they do. You definitely will have to take Bible Survey," she said, trying to
show care and understanding. She handed me a sheet of paper that read
"Bible Test Result 45%."

"Mrs. Hensley, I know there must be some reasonable explanation
for this outcome. I know that material. May I re-take the test?" I asked.

"No. You need to take the result back across the street so the registrar
can help arrange your course load," she said, as she directed me away from
her area. As I went back across the street to the Administrative Office, I
felt defeated and humiliated. Those results were wrong. I did not know
how to challenge the results, but knew I needed to do so. It would not
hurt me to take a Bible Survey course; but right is right. As I entered the
Administrative Office, I felt I needed to seek a resolution that might
entail having to go to a higher administrator.

"Here is what is recorded as my score, but I know it is wrong," I said
as I handed it to the secretary.

"What do you mean it is wrong? You are not the first student to fail
that test," she said.

"I am the first to fail it when I know I passed it with flying colors,"
I responded.

"Are you sure?" she asked.

"I am sure. I don't want to make any waves my first day on campus;
but I know something has to be wrong," I tried to clarify my position.

"Who administered the test?" she asked.

"Her name is Mrs. Hensley."

"Oh, she has been gone for a semester. This is her first day back. You are the first person this semester to take the test from her. Let me call her and see if we can get to the bottom of your test result," she said, while smiling at me. She picked up the phone and called. I could hear the two talking.

"Which test did you give him?" I heard her ask.

"Does it have a 67 or 68 in the upper left corner of the first page?" She waited to hear the answer.

"That is the correct test. We changed test questions this summer. Now, look at the answer sheet. How is it marked at the top left side?" Again, there was silence. The silence was lasting longer than before. "That is the wrong answer sheet. We changed tests and answers this summer. Both test and answers should have been changed. Can you go to the cupboard and see if you find the answer sheet labeled 68?" she asked, in a respectful tone. Longer silence.

"Yes, that would be the one to use this semester. Can you regrade his test using the correct answer sheet and call me with the results?" I looked very confused.

"We change the test each summer, so the test answers don't get out. The questions are similar; but we rearrange the order, so it is always different. It should only take a couple of minutes to get the results. Why don't you have a seat out in the lobby, and I will come and get you when the new results are provided to me." I walked out into the lobby and sat on the sofa. Soon I was motioned back into the registrar's office.

"Well, I guess God is looking after you and you have come to the right place. The result of the test when graded with the correct answer sheet shows you earned 99 out of 100. Is that more to your liking?" she asked, with a big smile.

"It's not that I am opposed to taking an extra class, but I needed the validation of what I actually earned," I said, as I jumped for joy. We then chose my semester courses which included Psychology 1A, History 1A, The Pentateuch, The New Testament, Old Testament Characters, and The Life of Jesus.

I was given my dorm room number and key and was told I was ready to start on Monday. The map would help me determine where each class was to be held and I was given instructions to go and find the location before classes started next week. I went out to Marilyn's car and waited for her to return so I could get my possessions. She had already moved her things from her car to her room. My bags were in the back seat of her car. She returned and asked if I wanted her to drive me up the hill to my dorm. I insisted it was not necessary.

I took my bags from the back seat and walked up the hill. The three-story building was the largest building on campus. There were many more men at the college than women. I saw a sign directing new students to enter from the side entrance. Of course, it was up at the top of the hill and to the backside of the building. My room was 207. It was hard to focus. I was not quite prepared for this undertaking. I opened the door to the dorm and walked down a very long hallway. The second floor was accessed from this side of the building. I found room 207 on the left side, facing the mountains. I put the key into the door and opened it. I looked at two large picture windows straight ahead. There was a very large piece of furniture in the middle of the room, in front of the windows, that had two desks on each side. It was one piece of wood with four desktops, drawers, and a place for your textbooks to be easily accessed. There were four chairs, one for each desk. To the right and to the left were two closets. One for each of the four people who would be sharing this space. There was a four-foot wall on each side of the entry where bunk beds had been placed, two on each side of the room. Again, there was storage area over each bed. There were no curtains on the windows or anything that provided privacy. Since I was the first and only person at this time, I decided I wanted the lower bunk to the immediate right as you entered the room. I also claimed the closet on the same side closest to the beds. The closets were quite large. The bottom section had lots of storage and drawers that could be used for storing anything you wanted out of sight. I placed my four shirts, two pairs of pants, two pairs of shoes, underwear, toothbrush, deodorant, aftershave, pen, pencils, a ream of lined paper, and my Bible into the closet. There was much room for growth.

Marilyn's parents had provided me a gift box that Marilyn brought to me about thirty minutes after I had walked up to the dorm. I saw her waving at me to come out to the car. Women were not allowed to enter the men's dorm under any circumstance. It was grounds for dismissal from the college.

I went out to meet her. "Mom and Dad wanted me to give this to you as a gift from them because they want you to know how proud they are of you and they thought this would come in handy this semester," she told me. I thanked her and walked back into the room with the box. It contained sheets, two blankets, washcloths, towels, soap, and a fifty-dollar bill.

One by one my three roommates showed up over the weekend. One was from Oregon. Allen was quiet and very much into the outdoors. He was quick to share with me that the only reason he was at Bethany was because his parents were forcing him to go to college for at least one year.

After that time, he was free to do whatever he wanted. Roommate two was Harlan, who had curly blonde hair and was a musician. He played the bass. He informed me he wanted to become a music minister for a church. The last roommate to join us was Rich and he was. He had an incredible personality. From the moment you met him, he was full of life, humor, and had communication skills I had never heard before. When Rich entered a room, no other person mattered. All the energy was directed not only at him, but from him toward you. He could make you feel important. By his fourth trip from his car (new and red) parked directly outside our room so he could make sure it was protected, he wanted to know if anyone wanted to help him bring the remainder of his stuff into our room. When neither of the other two responded, I got up from my bed and walked with him to his car.

He started the conversation. "My parents are older. I have a half-brother from my dad's first marriage. I am my parents' only child. I won't say I am spoiled, but I don't have to worry about wanting something and it not being provided. They want me to get a college education and thought I should come to Bethany because it is only about an hour from our house, making it close enough if I need something, but allowing me to be independent when I choose to be," he said, as he handed me several boxes. I was trying to figure out how he had loaded all these items into his car.

"What do you plan to do after college?" I asked, as we walked back to the room.

"It doesn't really matter. I will probably do some type of sales. I am good at talking to people. I don't think I need a college education; but my parents want me to have one and I want to please them," he said, as we opened the door to the dorm. By this time, Rich had filled his closet.

"Do any of you have any extra room in your closet?" he asked, as he opened my closet without permission. He let out a huge joyful scream.

"Oh, my God, Ron, is this your closet? You have virtually nothing. Can I please use your closet also?" Without waiting for my answer, he had started moving clothes into my closet.

"Under one condition; I can wear anything that is housed on my side if it fits me," I demanded.

"It is a deal," said Rich. After several more trips for clothes, my closet was full, more than full; he had all his clothes arranged between our two closets into perfectly matched pairings: short-sleeved shirts, long-sleeved shirts, sweaters, pants, coats, and swimming apparel. He then took out a special box that had been placed in the middle of a larger box. It was a miniature television. I had never seen one so small. Rich announced to the three of us, "I know it is against the rules to have this in our room, but there are a couple of shows I cannot live without. Any one of you can use it; just don't get caught because the hall monitors will take it and not return it. It cost a lot."

During that semester, the floor monitor knocked on our door a couple of times when he thought he heard a television; but Rich had a special place at the bottom of his dirty clothes basket for it. He would race to cover it as one of us went and stalled for just enough time for Rich to hide it. The monitor was not going to stick his hands into someone's dirty laundry. He did ask us to open drawers, cupboards, and closets. The television was never confiscated.

CHAPTER TWO

I knew when I arrived at Bethany that I had to get a job to support myself. I learned that some of the other boys worked at McDonald's in Santa Cruz proper. At the time it was the busiest franchise in the corporation. Buses would pull up on their way up and down the California coast. I also learned that a small number of boys carpooled to their jobs in the city and that, for a small fee, I was welcome to go with them. Almost every shift found a few Bethany boys working there. I interviewed and got hired. Within two weeks I went from cleaning the grounds, washing down the inside and outside tables, and cleaning the equipment, including draining the fry machine and milkshake machines, to taking orders. All the time I had spent at the Snack Shack at Shafter High School paid off. The managers loved me. They started giving me the closing shift. What was great about that shift was at closing was that any burgers, fries, and shakes that had been made but not sold were dumped. I asked if I could take them back to the dorm instead of putting them in the trash. The manager gave me permission. It did not take long until we had hungry students waiting for us to arrive back at the dorms at closing time.

One night I was scheduled to close. It was the only night I can remember when I was the only "Bethany boy," as they called us, on that night shift. I did not have any transportation back to school. I called Bethany with the hopes of getting the switchboard to transfer my call to my room so I could ask Rich to come after me, but the switchboard was closed. I had borrowed a wool coat from one of the guys in the dorm because it had been extremely cold at night and I did not own a heavy coat. I started walking back to the college. I had walked more than seven miles on many occasions, but never on a night as cold as this. I had been walking for about two miles. I was on the freeway portion of Highway 17, which is the only road connecting McDonald's on Highway101 with Bethany. It was really cold out on the road and I felt miserable. It had started raining and was blowing directly into my face. I thought it might be better to walk backwards for a bit; but because I was walking on the side of the freeway, I decided it would be better to keep one foot in front of the other and imagine a safe warm and sunny beach as I walked.

Suddenly, I heard a car horn sound and I noticed colored lights flashing. I looked behind me and saw a police car pulling toward me. I heard a voice coming from the microphone attached to the car, it said, "Walk to the right side of the road and stop." I was hoping the policeman would give me a ride because it was really raining now. The officer rolled down his window.

"Where are you headed at this time of the night?" he asked.

"I am headed home. I live in the dorms at Bethany Bible College," I proudly proclaimed.

"Really?"

"Yes. I just finished my shift at McDonald's, and did not have any transportation tonight, to get home," I said, trying to clarify why I was outdoors in the rainy night.

"Would you like for me to take you to the college?" asked the officer. I could not control my excitement and joy for such a gracious offer.

"That would be wonderful. Praise God," I said.

"Indeed. Get in the back of the car," commanded the officer. He turned off the lights that were circulating red, white, and blue colors. I thought if he was going to be this caring, I needed to remember to thank him and to make sure he didn't have to do more than what was needed.

"You sure you are a student at Bethany? You don't really look like most of the students I have met," he commented.

"You probably don't meet them after a six-hour shift at McDonald's and walking back to the dorms because they could not get hold of any of their roommates to come after them when their shift was over," I explained. We were now arriving at the entry into Bethany Lane where all the beautiful homes are situated.

"You can let me off here at the bottom of the hill if you like. I really appreciate your assistance," I stated.

"Oh, no, that is not necessary. You know it is against the law to walk on the edge of the freeway in California, don't you?" he asked.

"That may be, but it is the only way to get home. No surface streets come out to the college. Again, I appreciate your bringing me this far." I tried complementing him.

"I wouldn't think of leaving you here. I want to see you get to your dorm," said the officer.

"That is way above and beyond the call of duty," I said. We drove up the hill. When we got towards the top and entered the campus, the officer again turned his lights on drawing attention to our entry into the college.

"Where do you live?" he asked.

"The men's dorm is at the top of the hill on the left side," I told him. By this time, several students were looking out their windows, some leaving the dorms and going into the street to see what was causing the fuss. We pulled up at the entrance to the dorm. Again, I thanked him for the lift. I saw him writing something. He asked me for my driver's license.

"I am going to give you a citation for walking on the freeway. You will have to appear in court within two weeks. Have I made myself clear?" he asked.

"What would you have done if this were the only way for you to get home?" I asked.

"I would not have broken the law. Doesn't Bethany teach you not to break laws?" he asked.

"I don't see how my walking home the only way possible is breaking the law," I responded. "Again, thanks for the ride and do what you have to do. I will take my chances with a judge." He was now letting me out of the back seat of the cruiser.

"I can handle this from here. I will call and see when I can go to court," I said in the calmest voice I could muster.

"I want to make sure you actually live here. Take me to your room," he said as he gently pushed me toward the entry to the dorm. By this time, several boys were looking out of their windows and some were coming out of the dorms to see what was going on. The lights on the car were still flashing. We walked down the corridor. When we got to room 207, I went to open the door, but it was locked. I knocked on the door. The door opened and Rich was standing in front of us. I had never been so glad to see anyone. The officer was now holding me from behind with both hands on my shoulders and he asked Rich, "Do you know this person?"

Rich must have thought this was all part of a joke and replied, "I have never seen this person before," very seriously. The officer suddenly moved to cuff me by placing my hands behind my back and was moving to put handcuffs on me when Rich realized this was not a joke.

"Yes, yes, of course he lives here. He has been at work at McDonald's. He is our roommate. His name is Ron Reel." The officer let loose of one of my wrists and was moving to take off the handcuff from the other.

"You are going to have to go into that room and show me something that is yours," he stated as he pushed me into the room. I walked to my desk. Here are three of my books. I have my name on the inside jacket of each one," I replied. The officer read the books and slowly retreated toward the door.

"Next time call a friend or wait until someone comes after you. If you are going to work that far from the college, you might consider getting a car." He turned, walked back down the hall, and got back to his car where he hit the siren one last time, waking up others who had not been awakened by his lights. He drove away.

When I knew he was gone, I turned to Rich. "You knew I was working tonight. When I didn't come home, you could have come to get me," I shouted.

"I am not your personal chauffeur," Rich said, as he went to the closet and put on one of his hats, which resembled what a driver might wear.

"You are going to have to take me to the courthouse because I cannot chance another ticket before I see the judge," I commanded my new chauffeur. On Monday I called the courthouse and scheduled my appearance. Rich took me that Friday. The court appearance was set at 3:00 p.m. This was the first time I had any conflict with the law. I had never been inside a courtroom. I heard from my older brothers what it was like; but for someone who feared a parent raising his voice almost as much as being whipped, a courthouse was very intimidating. I noticed many people sitting in the court. I could not imagine this many traffic violations in Santa Cruz. We sat down and waited for my case to be called.

I was dumbfounded with some of the cases that came before my case. One lady was pulled over for driving while she was putting eyeliner on her eyes while driving on the freeway. She was steering with her legs and not using her hands. It was all I could do not to laugh. One man had been given thirty tickets for parking his car in a red zone. His defense was that he was color blind and could not see the red color. I guess he could not read either. A college student from Cabrillo had been pulled over for swerving in and out of lanes while he took out and put back in his contact lens. The judge seemed to be getting more firm with each decision. None of these people who had been charged were found innocent. Finally, my name was called. I moved to the designated area. The officer had told me he would see me in court, but when the clerk was asked where the officer was by the judge, he was told he had not appeared. The judge read my charge.

"You have been given a ticket for walking on the side of the freeway. Would you care to explain?" asked the judge.

I took a deep breath and began to explain, "Your honor, I am a student at Bethany Bible College. My mother died during the summer and my father kicked out the three of us still living at home. The pastor of my church was responsible for my getting a combination grant and loan scholarship so I could go to college and eventually make a difference in our society. I plan to become either a minister or a teacher. I don't have a car and I am responsible for meeting my own financial obligations. Usually, I can ride back and forth to the college with other students who work at McDonald's. This one night, there were no other Bethany students working. There is only one way to the college, and it forces one to travel down the freeway. There is no side street that gets you to Scotts Valley. I was not disturbing anyone. I was not hitchhiking. I was not littering. I was just trying to get back to the dorm so I could finish my homework and prepare for my exams. The officer turned on his siren and lights and took me through the campus so anyone and all wanting to see a sideshow had the opportunity."

The judge looked around. He then said, "I hope that everyone in this courtroom listened to this young man. He is an example of what is right for our country. What kind of an officer would issue a citation to someone trying to become a productive member of our society? You are the hero of my court today, young man. Watch what I am going to do right now." He took the complaint, tore it in half, crumbled it, and threw it on the floor.

"Rest assured, Mr. Reel, if you were my son, I would be proud of your work ethic and drive. Should you find yourself needing to walk home again to the college; walk proudly and with the knowledge that if any insane officer ever cites you again for such courage and fortitude, I personally will call him into my court and embarrass him before a courtroom full of people. I am the only traffic judge; and you have a free pass anytime you need it. You may leave now; this ridiculous and frivolous citation has been overturned, expunged, and will go down in the history of my court as the most reckless abuse of power and harassment by an officer who has ever come before me. Thank you for being the man you are and will become."

"No, your honor. You are my hero. You have stood up for the marginalized and usually invisible members of our society. I would be proud to be your son."

I turned to face Rich. His wide grin said it all. His smile reached from one side of his face to the other.

"You did it," he said.

"No, the judge did it. He is my hero."

CHAPTER THREE

Every class during the third week of the semester began with the professor announcing the importance of all freshmen attending an all-school rally, Friday afternoon at 3:00 p.m. The professors read the announcement sternly, stressing that the meeting was mandatory. By my third class of the week, I had almost memorized it. I could have done a better job at interpretive reading than the professors who were complying with an administrative requirement and did not seem very happy to be doing so. Only one of my professors asked if there were questions after making the announcement.

"Any questions about the time, place, or purpose?" Professor Oni asked.

I could not let this opportunity pass. "This is the third time I have heard this announcement. It has been presented in the same way. You are the first to ask for questions. Have you attended it in the past; why is the meeting so important; and what happens if we can't meet at that time?" I asked.

Professor Oni thought for a minute before delivering his answer. "I have been here almost twenty years. It is perhaps one of the most inspirational and uplifting things we do at the college. Every faculty member, staff support person, administrator, and freshman student gather in one place to share the purpose, goals, and reason for attending this institution. There is praise singing, testimonials, and a message that is usually designed to make us think about why we decided to become associated with a religious institution regardless of the major we chose," he explained. I was impressed. The college would have been better served had they asked him to go to each freshman class and share that message, instead of having an announcement read by someone who did not share his passion.

"What should I expect?" I asked.

"You will never forget the excitement that begins to grow just by being assembled together, moves to inspirational singing from various individuals and groups, and climaxes with testimonials as to why God has directed students like yourself to come and be educated here. They will touch your inner core," he concluded.

"I cannot wait. You make it sound worthwhile," I responded.

Anticipation began mounting as the week progressed. Some of the older guys in the dorm indicated to me how worthwhile it had been for them. They also told me that the high point of the afternoon would be a special guest appearance by one of the professors, singing a song that would take our breaths away because of his or her history and voice. They refused to tell me who the singer would be.

I kept guessing to myself which professor I thought would be the soloist. First, I thought about my psychology professor, who was a rather heavy person. He looked like he could sing an operatic aria, but his speaking voice was soft and somewhat whiny. Then I thought my history professor might be the mystery guest. She was one of only a few female professors at the college. She had revealed during the introduction portion of class on the first day that she had thought about pursuing a job in the entertainment industry at one time, before God called her to teach. I continued to speculate about the others. I was confident it was not the physical education professor. He only had a bachelor's degree. He had been coaching basketball and volleyball for the past twenty years. He could have been a major professional basketball player had he not gotten hurt during his final collegiate season. He had experienced a car accident that had caused several years of hospitalization, rehab, and pain management. He revealed that at one point he was told he would never walk again. He had told us that he was a walking example of God's grace and healing power. Even though he was quite tall, his nickname was Shorty. Coach Short is how everyone addressed him. He had shared his desire to do nothing but coach sports. He was proud of his many league championship banners that were placed around the gym. I finally gave up trying to figure out who the mystery person would be. I would just wait and see.

Finally, the day arrived and as Rich and I left our dorm room to walk to the gym, we talked as we walked. I started the conversation: "Rich, what really made you decide to come to Bethany? I have noticed you don't study that much. Usually you have some magazine inside your book when you are supposed to be studying," I prodded.

"Really, do you think I am reading magazines instead of studying? You, who are wearing one of my nice sweaters right now as we descend on the masses, have the nerve to ask such a question?" Rich smiled as we continued to walk. At first, I thought I had caused what might become an uncomfortable situation, but he continued, "I thought I had disguised that routine perfectly at home. I have always been an average student; but I would like to help people visit the entire world. I want to plan trips, coordinate excursions, and provide education about many cultures with cheap tickets available for different types of cultural experiences."

"You mean you want to be a travel guide?" I asked.

"Much more than that. I want to own a travel agency. I will have to explain it to you when we get back to our room, if you would like," Rich said as he put his hand on my shoulder. "Let me guide you along this uneven path so you don't fall and put a hole in that expensive sweater that looks quite nice on you," he said in a protective brother's voice. I already liked him. He was two years older than the other freshmen. He had all the good qualities I had wanted my twin to possess. He always looked like a professional model from his hair-blown precision cut, to his matching shirt, sweater, and color coordinated pants, down to his shiny shoes. He always wanted to be on the go. When I would tell him, that I had no money to go into town to eat, go to the beach, or even to go body surfing, he would say, "Did I ask if you had money? I just asked if you want to go," he would say as he smiled and did his best to upset my study routine and work ethic. It was 1968 and his parents sent him a check that arrived every Wednesday in the amount of $50.00 for spending money. We walked on toward the gym.

"Why don't you just tell your parents what you want to do?" I asked.

"Because I promised them that I would give this college experience one year. After this year I can decide to return to school or to do what I want. This is my gift to them," he said.

"You know they are going to back you with any decision you make," I predicted.

"I know and I am grateful because they have always allowed me to do what I wanted. Mom has one of her maids making us curtains to provide some privacy for our dorm room. I will be bringing them back when I return Sunday. I am going home for the weekend right after this assembly. By the way, I have told Mom and Dad how impressed I am with your being here on your own and they told me they like you even though they have not met you yet," Rich shared. I was anticipating a new or different car when he returned. Each week he would come back to the campus with a different car. It was unusual. I thought perhaps his parents owned some type of car dealership.

"Rich, you are one of the luckiest people I know. Your parents love you. You can decide to study hard or not. You have an OK personality, but most of all I enjoy being around you because you are fun. I have a need for that because I did not have much fun growing up," I shared.

We arrived at the gym. People were entering the building from both the front and the two side entrances. Rich directed me to begin walking up the bleachers.

As we walked up the stairs he spoke again, "Let's sit right in the middle section where we can have the best view of the speakers. Follow me and you will enjoy the service far more than if you just go where you are headed," he called out to me and a couple of other people who thought he was talking to them. After a few minutes, the ceremony started. I did not know or recognize the first speaker. Later, in my speech career, I would learn this person is what is known as the moderator. His purpose was to introduce the first major speaker. In this case, they had him lead us in prayer. It was amazing to see all the students, faculty, and staff bow their heads and be in one accord for one moment in time. I looked around to see how other people were reacting. I was grateful to be in the midst of a collegiate life that had Godly principles at its core. As I stood there thinking about what I was hearing in the prayer, I realized how lucky I had been to have so many great teachers and clergy support me. As he finished the prayer, the great reveal began.

"It is now my honor and privilege to introduce someone whom every single person here knows and loves. Yes, all of you here today know this person. Sit back and let God share a message through one of the greatest singers I have ever heard. Coach Short, please come and minister. The one person I thought it would never be was the person who stood before us in a blue double-breasted blazer, white shirt, red and white tie, navy blue pants, and shiny black shoes. He looked like he had been taken off the cover of a fashion magazine. He certainly was not the gym coach standing before us in his sweats. Once he began singing, he shocked all of us. He was as good a soloist as I had heard live or on television. He appeared to have at least a four-octave range. At times he was singing in his lower registry, then suddenly he would float up higher than any tenor could sing. His song was about what amazing grace God has for each of us. I looked for his accompanist, but the piano bench sat unoccupied. He was singing live but was using an accompanying tape. You could hear the orchestral instruments that gave this type of singing a feeling of listening to an actual record, but made it more interesting by having a live singer. By the end of the song he was singing loud and clear; he sustained the last note for what seemed like a minute. Immediately, the entire audience was on their feet. Coach Short had accomplished his task.

Once the audience calmed down, coach spoke, "Welcome to Bethany. Many of you know I was a student here a long time ago. I call this place home. You are sitting in my house. I didn't build it, but God lets me and you live here. Be humble, give Him credit for your success, and most importantly, listen for God to direct your choices. We are His ambassadors. We will be judged by our actions and voices. Now it is my honor to present to you the greatest ambassador to the world this college has ever had; song scholar, author, evangelist, my friend, Reverend Dr. Arnold Cotton, who wants to welcome you and give some of you an opportunity to share why you are here," coach said, as he moved away from the stage and handed the microphone to Dr. Cotton.

He waited for the applause to die down and spoke, "God moves us every single day in various ways. He helps us be at certain places each day where someone is hurting, needs encouragement, has a special request that needs to be honored, or simply needs us to listen as a dedicated friend. He also gives us talents we don't even know we possess. If you notice the piano, it sits on stage without anyone playing today. The person scheduled to play, my personal pianist, became ill at the last minute. God has told me someone is sitting in this audience who should leave his or her seat and come to the stage and play for us. I am being told you know how special you are to God. He has helped you overcome many obstacles and has a special path ready for you. You have never played the piano, but God is the maker of all, and He is telling me He will give you the ability to play any song perfectly, if you step out in faith and move to the piano. Let us all bow and close our eyes. No one looking around. I know you are a male; you almost did not come to our college this year; you sing but have never played the piano. God is calling you. Step out in faith," he demanded. I felt like he was talking to me. I had been given many people who helped me overcome obstacles, I sang; not half as good as Coach Short, and I had never had the opportunity to learn how to play the piano. I had heard of people just waking up and knowing how to play any song they heard. I did not see myself as that talented. I wanted to step out in faith but could not.

Dr. Cotton began to speak again, "You are here right now. However, you have not grown enough in God to trust his ever powerful being. It has passed." Just as he uttered those words, the side door to the gym opened and closed with a sharp sound. As the person walked to the stage, Dr. Cotton introduced him.

"Ladies and gentlemen, the pianist who was originally scheduled to play, has made it after all. Let us sing some praises to God," he instructed us. We sang a few choruses that any churchgoer knows. I don't remember much more that happened. Some of the students gave testimonials as to how and why they were attending Bethany.

I was very mad at myself. God had spoken to me to get up out of my seat and go play the piano. I just did not have enough belief in myself or faith in God. I felt that I let God down. It would be a few years before I would ever forgive myself. During this time, I wondered if it had been set up to have the pianist late to provide for someone who felt unqualified to find the strength they needed to perform before a large audience. Because of the statement about never having played the piano before; that should have eliminated people who played but did not think they were that good from jumping from their seats. I never shared my unwillingness to obey God with anyone for at least three decades. I did not have the strength to step out then, but I would step out in many instances in the future.

* * * * *

By the end of my fourth week at Bethany, many of the students were forming various groups that would help them meet their obligation to take the gospel message into the community. The college expected each student to participate in at least five religious services each week: two services on Sunday, one on Wednesday evening, and at least two other services of their choice. Some students were marketing themselves to others, while some were joining forces with newly met or ongoing friends to accomplish the "ministry" aspect of the social commitment to "Take the message of God into all parts of the world."

Rich, Harlan, and I decided to form a singing group that would be contemporary, relevant, and much more appealing to people our age than some of the previous groups we had heard about. We needed at least four people. We especially desired a deep voice that could make any song's lyrics stand out. I had met another freshman, Jeremy, who was seventeen, in one of my religion classes. He was very thin, tall, and weighed about 140 pounds. One day after class we were talking about the assignment that had been given to us to make the message of Jesus apply to college students, when one of the girls in our class came over to where we were standing and said to Jeremy, "I really enjoyed your solo Sunday at Santa Cruz Assembly. I could have never sung before a congregation of at least 1,000 people. I have never heard such a deep singing voice. How do you find that registry?" They say God moves in mysterious ways, perhaps, He had moved Jeremy into our group. I told Jeremy about what we were planning, and he agreed to check us out.

We felt the sound of our music needed to be different from that which most quartet type of groups provided; but, in addition to the sound, the name would need to be modern to bring a young group of converts to know Jesus in a special way. There had been groups like "The Gospel Singers," "Sidewalk Singers," "Hillside Worshipers," "New Life Singers," "United Voices," and even Bethany's own "The Bethanaires." We wanted something different.

I don't remember who actually came up with the name for our group; it may have been Rich; but I know we all instantly thought it would be revolutionary. We knew it would pop. We felt the young hippy-type person wanting to be carefree and seeking unconditional love in the world during 1968 would appreciate and be intrigued by our name and want to come and hear what we had to say; I mean, what we had to sing. Our official name would be *"The Sons of Bathsheba."* We would shorten it to *"The SOB's."* Most people had some understanding of the stories from the Bible and knew about the scandalous relationship between David and Bathsheba, a married woman. Certainly, we were relying on the more accepted social connotation of what people thought when they heard or saw *SOB* in writing, to provide a shock or, a curiosity factor. We were performing "rock religion" ten years before it materialized as a legitimate form of religious entertainment.

We practiced for several weeks on campus in the late evenings at Craig Chapel. We would meet there because it had a great sound system and had an actual stage with a piano. Some other students started gathering in the back of the chapel during our practice sessions to hear what we were doing. We tried to feature traditional four-part harmony at some point during every song. We also wanted unusual arrangements of songs which would feature either high tenor or low bass solos, which people would not associate with the song because of how they had heard it sung in the past. Our goal was to provide entertainment to a newer generation seeking an edgy entry into the world of religious music. Having our peers sitting in the back of the chapel fed our egos. They shared with us how much they liked the new sound of old songs.

We created one hundred flyers for our first gig to be held on campus at Craig Memorial Chapel the following Saturday evening. We distributed the flyers to our fans who had been coming to our rehearsals. We explained that they were to give the invitation only to people they thought would enjoy this new type of religious songfest. We further explained that only those with the secret invitation in hand would be admitted to the performance. Each flyer would admit one or two people. We felt this would allow the invited guest to bring a date but would not result in too many people attending our first concert. By limiting the number of flyers, we were also controlling the total number of people allowed into the chapel according to the fire marshal and evacuation codes. We were trying to observe all the rules concerning performances.

By Thursday's practice, more and more fans were showing up. Many stayed until we were finished with rehearsal to share with us the number of students to whom they had given the flyers. We were feeling confident that our hard work, creativity, and new edge approach to Christian music was about to pay off. We decided to forgo dressing alike and instead would show up in our regular school clothes. We wanted the music to be the star of the evening.

Friday morning our hall monitor, a student resident responsible for overseeing our floor and the activities of student life in the dorm, posted a letter on our door. Rich discovered the letter as he was leaving for the showers and his early morning ritual. He came back in, woke us, and began to read the letter: "Dear Mr. Lee, Reel, and other members of a singing group who have not had their name officially approved by the college. You are hereby required to attend a meeting with college president Dr. Cotton. This appointment has been scheduled for 1:30 p.m. today. This meeting is mandatory. Please do not be late."

We did not know what to think of this request for an audience with the president of the college. I pulled out the paperwork the college had provided regarding formation of performance guidelines and approval procedure protocol. The rules and regulations stipulated the college needed to sign-off on your purpose, name, and type of ministry. We knew our type of ministry (singing), purpose (entertainment and conversion to Christianity) would be approved by any rational person. The only detail that might be questioned would be our name. It might be too avant-garde for some. We agreed that I would be our spokesperson at the meeting.

At exactly 1:30 p.m. that afternoon, the four of us, who had been sitting outside the president's office, were escorted inside. I felt like I had been sent to the vice principal's office for some type of disciplinary action.

President Cotton greeted us, "Gentlemen, please be seated. I want to begin first by thanking each of you for attending our college. We take great pride in providing a first-rate education for both the soul and the personal well-being of students, who leave our campus and go into the world to take God's message where it is needed. I have had several conversations with some of your fans, who are quite taken with your talents, creativity, and showmanship. It appears from their evaluations and support; you are quite talented and might have an opportunity to excel in musical theater. There is one problem. Your name is not acceptable for this college. We will not have a singing group called, "The SOB's." It sounds too worldly."

I thought it now appropriate for me to share our thought processes and creativity for our choice of name. "Dr. Cotton, if you would allow me to share with you why we feel the name is appropriate. Our official name is "The Sons of Bathsheba." We are each a son of someone, and we took this Biblical name to be reflective of being born to no one person, but being sons of all women everywhere, forgiven or yet to be forgiven. Our message, through our name, is absolute and unconditional acceptance of all," I claimed.

"Well, I must say I am impressed by this attempt to justify such a creative name choice. It is the initials that appear on your flyer that have me troubled. "The SOB's" connotes to me something other than what you suggest and brings to my mind a meaning that will not come from this college while I am president. Had you turned your paperwork into the college as directed, before you started publicizing your group, we would not be having this meeting. You may have your group, but you will change the name. I like your gumption, spunk, and creativity. Now put it in a direction that will benefit you, our campus, and God. I am going to destroy this official complaint, and nothing will appear in your student files because I know you are going to follow my request. By the way, I want you to collect those flyers tonight, bring them to my secretary on Monday, and we will destroy them for you. All evidence of this will be gone. You are dismissed," he said. We left his office. That night we collected all the flyers, ending the singing career of the best named and most creative group ever to sing at Bethany. Well, at least, that is the way I remember it.

CHAPTER FOUR

Rich, Allen, Harlan, and I decided one afternoon to go to the beach at Santa Cruz. Rich asked us to go with him to get some sun. I had never been to a beach, so I was eager to go. Allen, the lightest complexioned of the four of us, came from Oregon, where he often joked, they had temperatures over 80 degrees fewer than seven days a year. I did not own a swimsuit, but Rich had several in our shared closet. He picked out the one he wanted to wear and threw a blue suit to me. Harlan decided to wear a pair of cut-off jeans. Allen, who was much skinner than the rest of us, surprised us by wearing the skimpiest bathing suit I had ever seen. It looked like a pair of underwear shorts that had shrunk. Rich had brought four beach towels from home. He asked if we had suntan lotion; none of us did. He went to his desk and opened one of the drawers. He brought out a bottle of suntan lotion made from coconut oil. We left our dorm room and jumped into Rich's car of the week. This time it was a convertible and Rich put the top down before we left the parking lot.

As we approached the Santa Cruz pier, I questioned the rest of them, "I have never been to a beach before today. What exactly are we going to do?" I asked.

"Well, we are going to begin by finding a nice sandy part of the beach near the water so we can bury ourselves in a comfortable bed-like setting. The sand will serve as a mattress. Our bath towels will serve as sheets on the bed of sand. We can take off our clothes, except for our suits, of course, and bask in the sun's rays. We will need to make sure to put on the lotion where our skin is exposed so we don't get sunburned. Each of you can put on your own lotion or we can help each other if you want." We were now parked, and Rich had put the top up on the car. We walked from the parking lot toward the beach, through an arcade and some buildings filled with gift shops, restaurants, and booths from which to purchase tickets for the amusement rides.

"Keep walking past all of these distractions," Rich commanded. We walked out of that area onto the beach. Rich led us to a place he determined was just right for our afternoon break. As we peeled off our clothes and placed them on our towels, I noticed for the first time the different physical make-up of my roommates. Allen was tall, not muscular at all, and was so skinny he could hardly be seen lying in the sand. Harlan was larger boned. He did not work out and had a slightly bulging belly. He was not fat, but some sit-ups would have helped his physique. Rich seemed very fit; but was, perhaps, the hairiest person his age I had ever seen. There was more hair on his back than most men had on their chests. The hair on his chest and stomach was so thick one could not see his skin.

Harlan looked at Rich and said, "You think you are related to the apes?" Rich responded to this statement quickly, "This is what is called masculine attraction. Don't be jealous. I will serve as a magnet to draw attention to us from any females walking by."

"The only girls who are going to want to see what I am seeing now will be apes or gorillas who have escaped from the zoo," Harlan responded with a smile.

"You think I have too much hair? Can any man have too much hair?" asked Rich.

"You are what you are. We will get use to you being who you are. I will now call you "Harry" instead of Rich when we are in private. Harlan was a man of his word, and from that day on, Harlan always called Rich "Harry."

I had just made my first official body pose for sun worshiping. I was lying on my back with my legs spread and arms at my side when Rich spoke to me. I did not know if he were trying to deflect the conversation away from himself or if he were surprised by how I looked.

"Ron, did you pile up some sand under your body to raise your body up above us?" Rich asked.

"No. What are you talking about?"

"Your chest is so large I cannot see Harlan or Allen. You must have put sand under your towel," he claimed.

"My chest is this size because of all my running I guess."

"It is massive. You make the rest of us look small," Rich said. I didn't know how to take this statement. I thought, perhaps, it was meant to be a compliment. Yet, I was not sure. Rich continued, "OK, enough talking, let's just relax, close our eyes, and enjoy the sun. About ten minutes later Rich interrupted our peace, reminding us to put on suntan lotion. As we did so, he pointed out areas where we may have missed covering some skin. It was now his turn to apply the lotion. I was next to him. I was not schooled in beach behavior, but I wondered whether someone this hairy could get a sunburn. He was lying face down with his backside up.

"Do you want me to put some of this lotion on your back?" I asked.

"That would be great. Be very careful; I am quite ticklish." I gently squeezed the lotion into my hands and spread it over his upper and lower back area. Rich thanked me when I was finished.

It took so much lotion to cover his backside and legs my hands were quite greasy when I finished. I excused myself and headed back toward the arcade to find a restroom or water fountain to wash my hands. As I approached the arcade, I noticed the restrooms just to the right of the entry. I went inside and washed the lotion from my hands. When I left the restroom and headed back to join my group, I saw a gift store with a pretty girl standing behind the counter. She was by herself. No one else was in the store. Our eyes met and she smiled at me. I walked closer to the entrance of the store. When I arrived at the door, I could see her name tag, "Patricia."

"Hi Patricia, I am Ron."

"I saw your group go out to the beach earlier. It is not a busy day. Are you a local or just visiting?" she asked.

"We are roommates from Bethany. None of us is from here. We decided to try out the beach. It is the first time I have ever been to any beach," I shared.

"It is a good day to get some rays. It is not too hot nor is it going to get cold soon. I am a student at UC Santa Cruz. I live with my parents. It is nice to meet another college student. Don't get many of them here. Most of my time is spent working at the counter here or studying in the library at school," she stated.

"Well, I better get back to the beach before my friends miss me," I said as I turned to go back to the beach.

"Well, I work Monday through Friday from 1:00 p.m. to 5:00 p.m. if you want to stop by and talk; or get something to eat after I finish my shift," she said with a great smile. I left thinking that she could possibly be flirting with me.

When I got back to the group, Rich asked, "Where have you been? Why did you leave? Did you have to go to the bathroom?" he asked.

"Yes, I had to go and wash off some of the massive amount of lotion I had to put on your body so you would not get sunburned, if the rays can penetrate through all your fur," I joked.

"Well, sit or lie down so you can enjoy this peaceful beach God has made just for us," Rich said.

"Besides, when I went to clean the lotion off my hands, I met a girl," I said, dangling this statement to see if I would get some reaction. Almost on cue, all three of them said:

"What did you just say?" asked Harlan.

"Did you say what I think you said?" asked Allen.

"Of all of us, you met a girl?" asked Rich. I waited just a couple of seconds before I started to describe what had just happened.

"As I was coming out of the restroom from washing my hands, I saw this very attractive girl standing behind a counter in the store across from the entry to the arcade. She smiled. I smiled. I approached the door and we began a conversation. It ended with my leaving; but she made it a point to let me know I could come back during her shifts and could ask her out. What do you think I should do?" I asked, hoping they all would tell me to go for it.

"Are you kidding? At the end of our time here today, go ask her out," commanded Harlan.

"I could go with you and she will probably want me instead," said Allen.

"If she does want to go out with you, I can be your driver and your dressing consultant," said Rich. After we had tanned on each side for another 25 minutes or so, we decided it was time to go back to the dorms. As we walked back to the arcade area, I saw there was a customer talking with Patricia. I motioned for the guys to go ahead to the car. I waited outside until the customer left. Then I went inside to talk to Patricia.

"I thought I might come by and ask what you are doing Friday after work," I told her.

"I hope to be spending the time with you. I am off at 5:00 p.m. Don't be late. We can get something to eat and maybe we can take a walk on the beach," she said.

"I will be here. See you then," I replied. I received advice from the three roommates for the next few days. Rich was willing to drive me and be my chauffeur, however, I really did not feel that would be a good move. Finally, Rich told me he would loan me his car for the evening and not tag along if I would tell him everything that happened on my date when I got home. We spent about a half hour on Friday with him showing me the equipment on his car and how to start, park, and lock it up. Neither of us wanted it stolen while I was responsible for driving it. Just before I left, Rich handed me a twenty-dollar bill and told me to not spend it all at one place.

I showed up at exactly 5:00 p.m. Patricia was waiting. Her replacement was behind the counter. Patricia was talking with her but standing where most customers would be found. She saw me and moved quickly toward the door; I waved to her. As she came out of the store, she moved to my side and put her hand and arm around my left arm as we walked down the hallway toward the ticket booth for the rides.

"Would you like to ride the Cyclone roller coaster before we go and get food?" she asked.

"Sure, I have never been on this type of ride before," I said as though it were not true; but it was very true.

"Well, then you are in for a treat. It is scary at a couple of places and I will probably scream, and grab hold of you," she said, as we moved to the other end where tickets to all the rides were sold. Once we got our tickets and were on the coaster, sitting side by side, we looked at each other. I put my arm around her shoulder. She took my other hand and squeezed it as the ride started. It was not long before she was screaming. Every time she screamed, she put her head in the middle of my chest and hugged me. As we rolled back into the station, she took my hand, and lifted it toward her face, and kissed my hand.

"That was fun," she said. We got off the ride and walked across the street to a small Mexican café and had dinner. We talked and stared into each other's eyes. Finally, after dinner, I asked, "Would you like to take a walk on the beach?" She did not take long to answer,

"I thought you would never ask." She started to run ahead of me holding my hand and forcing me to run somewhat to stay up with her. There were many people on the beach.

We had walked for about ten minutes when Patricia said, "I know this private beach where it would be just the two of us walking, if you want to go with me."

I thought for just a second. "If it is private, will we be trespassers?"

"I don't know of anyone ever being arrested. Come on, I will direct you. You do have a car, right?" she asked.

"I have a car. Let's go," I responded. We walked to Rich's car. She looked at it and said, "Not so shabby. I thought you might be from a family of some means, but this is very impressive." She came closer and snuggled and we kissed. I did not know what to say. This was not my car. I didn't want to mislead her. I hoped she didn't want me because she thought my family was wealthy. I had to say something.

"This is not my car. My roommate loaned me his car. I don't have one at this time; I am between cars," I said. This statement was truthful.

"Your roommate let you borrow this car?" she asked.

"Yes. He is a great guy. He goes home each week and brings back a different car. He is very generous," I said. We were now in the car and Patricia was directing me north on CA 101, just outside the city limits.

"Turn left here," she said while pointing to an entrance that had a very large sign stating it was private property and to enter at your own risk.

"Are you sure we won't get in trouble?"

"I would never ask you to do anything that might result in your being arrested or making the papers in a scandalous way," she said. We were parked and started walking down to the ocean. It was magical. The sand was smooth, and the moon was out, lighting our journey to the shore where land meets water. There were no houses, no other people, just the two of us.

"I hope no one drops by unexpectedly and catches us here without permission," I said, in a somewhat playful voice.

"I promise they won't. I can talk our way out of any objections," she said.

"It sounds like you have been here before," I observed.

"I have. My parents own this beach. They are out of town this weekend and I know they won't drive by. Our house is just up that hill and around the corner. This is our own space for as long as we want it tonight; and I think it is time you call me Patty," she said with a smile. We kissed and then we sat on a big rock for a while talking about our majors, likes and dislikes, music, aspirations, and even about our families. We snuggled and further warmed each other with a blanket that Rich had placed in the back seat of the car. I had a great time just being there in the moment, without trying to be impressive; instead, we just shared. Around 11:30 p.m. we left the beach and I drove her home. She was correct; it was up the hill and around the corner. It was one of the largest homes I had ever seen.

Patty and I promised each other to talk again soon. As I drove back to the dorm, I realized that wealth is not what one possesses but what one has in self-confidence and self-worth. Once I got back to my room, Rich and I shared my entire evening from the beginning, despite our two roommates, who kept saying, "Enough already."

Patty and I talked together a good number of times that semester. We had many more dates. In December, however, she informed me that she was transferring to USC. We wrote a couple times after she left, but we never saw each other again. I know whomever she finally decided to love is a better person because of meeting and sharing this world with her. I am sorry I never found anyone else like her. Most of the women I would meet at work wanted something from me that I could not give.

CHAPTER FIVE

Thanksgiving arrived almost too quickly. Rich and I had secured jobs at a local Christmas tree farm. We were responsible for bagging the tree in a protective cover after the client returned from cutting his/her own tree out in the tree farm. The tree lot had several sections with various types of trees and different sizes based on the age of the trees. The owner replaced each tree cut at the end of each season's cuttings. This process allowed for various heights and widths of trees to be available.

Rich took Wednesday and Thursday off. He was going to return late Thursday night, ready to work the weekend after Thanksgiving. I stayed and worked the pre-Thanksgiving sale Wednesday because I did not have a family to visit.

When I returned to the dorm, it was almost vacant. I ran into one of the guys who lived at the opposite end of our hall. I had seen him in my gym class, but we had not officially met. I waved and smiled. He waved as he was coming down the hall toward me.

"I thought I was the only person left here today," he said.

"No, I don't have a family to go home to this year. So, I decided to stay to earn some extra money at the Christmas tree farm. We officially open on Friday," I told him.

"I was going to stay and try to catch up on some of my classes, but my mother just called and begged me to come home. She will be very disappointed if I don't."

"If my mother were still alive, I would do whatever it took to get home to spend a day with her. You never know when she might be taken from you," I shared.

"I love my mother, but my father and I don't see eye to eye on much of anything," he said.

"I can identify with that," I said, as we were coming together almost midway between our respective rooms.

"My name is Lawrence Rogers," he said.

"I am Ron Reel. I do think we are members of the forgotten or overlooked Thanksgiving crowd," I stated smiling.

"My folks own a large farm in central California. I can probably make it home in four hours. Want to come with me to visit my folks and my little sister?" he asked.

"I think your parents want to spend some quality time with you. A tag-along may not be welcome," I suggested.

"If I agree to come home, I can bring ten people with me and they won't care. We can return right after lunch tomorrow so I can get you back for your job on Friday," he vowed. We quickly packed and made the trip to Lemoore, where I discovered his family's ranch was hundreds of acres in size.

When we arrived, we were met by his parents. Both were very well spoken and appeared caring and affectionate toward their son. We were shown into the kitchen, where the live-in cook had prepared several things for us to eat. After enjoying the snacks, we were ushered to our bedrooms. My guest room was the largest bedroom I had ever been in.

The next day at breakfast, the concerns expressed by Lawrence about his father began to show themselves.

"Ron, Lawrence says your parents are ranchers also; where, if you don't mind my asking, are they located?" he asked.

"I think you misunderstood, or I didn't make myself clear to your son. My parents worked in the fields. We did not own a farm," I said, trying to clarify my true position. Lawrence's mother tried to redirect the conversation.

"All aspects of farming must take place for farming to be successful," she said. "Someone must do the work that has to get done. Tell us what your plans are after graduating from Bethany," she requested.

I started to answer, but Mr. Rogers brought up a new issue, "In fact, you might be the first child of a laborer whom I have met who carries himself so well and dresses so nicely," he said. He continued, "What happened to you that set you apart from all the other field laborer children?" he asked.

"I had some wonderful teachers who took it upon themselves to challenge and educate me. I also had a wonderful minister who was a role model. I owe anything I become to others who taught me," I explained.

"Certainly, we could not prosper without the Mexicans, Negroes, and poor whites to work our fields. Right now, I am having to fight a rebellious group from the Delano area. Maybe you have heard of their leader, Cesar Chavez," he said. Lawrence's mom quickly injected herself into the conversation.

"Enough discussion about work items. Let's focus on celebrating why we are thankful and let our son share with us what he has learned at Bethany," she said. The conversation turned to college and related topics. The family tacitly agreed to discuss only why they wanted their son at Bethany, and the academic challenges the college was providing. Lawrence's father didn't have much to say from this point forward.

We left right after the Thanksgiving dinner which had been served at 1:00 p.m. sharp. Lawrence used my job as the reason we had to leave so early in the afternoon. After getting back to the college, I waited for Rich to return to our room. We needed to plan our weekend job schedule. It was a very cold weekend and very rainy to work outside at the tree farm. The horrible weather exacerbated the normal problems associated with the cutting of Christmas trees.

* * * * *

During the next week I felt I was getting ill. I didn't know what it was, but I was not improving. By the end of the next weekend, which happened to be the last week of classes before finals week, I became so sick I could not get up out of bed. Rich called home and his mother told him to take me to the emergency room at the Santa Cruz Hospital, where I learned I had contracted the Hong Kong flu and needed medications and bedrest. The only time I left my dorm room during finals week was to take my examinations.

The college had a campus-wide contest for the room decorations that best exemplified the Christmas Spirit. Rich brought many branches from the tree farm home. He decorated our room with fresh tree limbs, created a nativity scene, and placed electric Christmas lights around and over the foliage. I was in bed when the judges toured our room. We placed third.

The campus closed for Christmas break. A girl Rich liked and dated a couple times named Lynette was from Bakersfield. She drove a

Volkswagen. She told me I could ride home with her if I wanted to visit my sister Nellie who also lived in Bakersfield. That car had so little power, we barely made it up to the top of a couple of the hills between Bethany and her home.

When I returned to my dorm room at the end of Christmas break, the only missing roommate was Rich. Finally, he pulled up in front of our window and started honking the horn of a blue Mustang. It really looked smart, sexy, and appeared to be brand new. He motioned for me to come out and meet him. I imagined he needed help bringing in items his mother sent back to the college after his visit home. I let him know how much I liked this car. I told him I liked it the best of all the cars he had driven this past year. I even told him that he should keep this car permanently and not bring any others to campus.

Once we got settled into the room and organized all the booty he brought from home, Rich said: "My mom and dad want to talk to you on the phone today. They have sent me with this contract they want you to examine and sign. It will allow you to become the owner of a car. They want to finance a car for you and will allow you to make payments to them at the rate of twenty-five dollars per month with no interest until it is paid in full," he said handing me a letter.

"I don't understand," I said, looking at him in a very confused manner.

"They are going to give you a car, pay the insurance for a year, and have you make payments to them of only twenty-five dollars per month until it is paid off," he said, again trying to stress the three parts of the contract I needed to understand.

"What kind of a car? I am sure they don't own anything from the 1950's that I can afford to pay them for that is good enough to drive. Rich, why me? Why are they willing to help me?"

"They are my parents, and they want to try to help you," he said smiling

"I don't know what to say. Perhaps we can go into town to a couple of the used car lots and find something I can afford," I said.

"Why are you talking about going into town?" Rich asked.

"We need to go find some type of car that is between a clunker and a car that will run most of the time," I said.

"Just finish reading the letter," he demanded. I continued reading. The car they were offering to sell me was the blue 1966 Mustang, which Rich had just shown me.

"Richard. I can't accept this!" I said, not knowing what else to say.

"They have made up their minds. Let's get them on the phone so you can thank them, and I won't have to continue to be your driver," he kidded me.

* * * * *

By the third week of my second semester, I decided I should try to get a job doing hair. A new hair salon was opening in Scotts Valley. I went into the salon and saw a woman who looked like she was in her late thirties or early forties. She was hanging a few pictures of current hair styles on one of the walls. She looked up and turned to face me.

"Hi, I am Ron Reel and I am a student at Bethany Bible College. I have recently gotten my license and now have transportation and would like to begin my professional career in hair styling, which will assist my paying the costs associated with attending college. Do you have any openings? If you do, can we discuss the terms of employment? I am sure I can be a successful addition to your staff," I said.

"Right now, there is only me. My husband and I just moved here, and I am trying to finalize the interior of the shop. We don't have a clientele yet; you will have to grow your own from scratch. You will not be a salaried employee. You will make only what you earn here in the salon. I will provide the colorings and perms at no cost to you; however, you will be responsible for setting your own fees so we both make a decent margin on each of the services you provide. Your split will be seventy percent of what you charge. As a man, you will most likely be able to charge more for your services than I can charge for mine. We will put a special advertisement on our window display letting everyone know your name and that we have both male and female stylists," she declared.

"You don't know yet if I can style or cut," I said.

"If you just finished school recently and you are here in this well-to-do area seeking work, either you are a great stylist, or you are the world's bravest person, who won't last long. I am willing to bet you will be a great addition to my business," she concluded.

"I get to set my own fees. They will be higher than yours," I declared.

"Each of us is an independent contract employee. We can charge what we wish," she said.

"I want my fees to be set at twenty-five dollars per haircut and twelve dollars per hair styling, sixty dollars for perms and hair coloring, eighty dollars for bleach and frostings," I said, knowing that these prices were extremely high.

"I will make a chart with your name and your fee schedule. Do we have a deal?" she asked, reaching out to shake my hand and confirm our agreement. I started officially the next day. We had cards made for me to give out at social functions and to clients once they had made an appointment. Within a week, I was making more money daily than I had been making at McDonald's weekly.

* * * * *

One of the highlights of my second semester classes was my enrollment in a public speaking course. I felt it would help me hone my skills and at the same time show off just how much I already knew. The college president's daughter was also enrolled in the class. The instructor was twenty-three years old; he had only had a BA, and he was also the choir, piano, and fine arts instructor. As the semester progressed, I realized he did not know much about speech. He was training on the job. Also, he agreed with whatever the daughter of the president said; he always acknowledged her answers as being correct when many times they were wrong. I went to him halfway through the semester to voice my concerns about what was happening during class and showed him the book, which contradicted much of what he had said. The meeting did not go well for me.

Mr. Odel had these words to express his position and how he felt about me: "I did not want to teach speech. I was told I would have to do this so I would have a full load and be considered full-time faculty. I am learning as much as you are this semester. I am not willing to fight the president by contradicting his daughter in class. I feel that what she brings up always make sense. Frankly, I don't know if you will ever make an outstanding public speaker, the kind we need in our line of ministry.

Ministers often speak from a written manuscript. Many times, however, it appears that you are simply relying on impromptu remarks," he told me.

I was shocked to learn he did not think I had what it took to be an outstanding public speaker. I had prided myself on my accomplishments in high school. I began to question myself and my ego became deflated. Mr. Odel was young, talented, gave outstanding piano recitals, and sang beautifully. He would not say something to hurt me deliberately. He must have thought he was trying to help me.

* * * * *

Around the eighth week of classes, I began thinking about what had transpired the year before concerning losing Momma and all that I had endured since. I found myself depressed and often crying uncontrollably. The reality of the loss of my immediate family was taking its toll on me. I could not concentrate on my studies. I lost interest in attending class and participating in classroom discussions, and I was not completing my assignments in a timely manner. I excelled in my hair styling job because I could be the lead actor; I wanted the people I helped by styling their hair to see me as a great cosmetologist. At college, I had to be myself. I was convinced that no one cared that I was alive or that I was the first in my family to attend college. I felt invisible. Perhaps naysayers like Mr. Odel were correct in their assessment of my true potential. I had developed such a deep depression that I found myself wishing I had never left the Bakersfield area. I felt I did not belong and was not able to compete with smarter students. I closed myself off to everyone including my roommates. Only Rich would not allow me to feel sorry for myself. He insisted that he and his family would never waste time on a person who could not respond to some adversity or temporary setbacks. His constant encouragement and suggestions that I needed to help him with his studies paid off and helped save me. Rich brought light back into my life. Unfortunately, by the time I overcame the dark abyss of negative thought and stopped feeling sorry for myself, it was too late for me to salvage my grades for that semester. Of my six classes, I only received one grade of "C." The rest were below that mark. I was told I could retake the classes in which I did not do well in the fall (paying for them again); and if I earned a grade of "C" or higher, only that grade would be counted when it came to calculating grade point averages for academic performance.

As the semester ended, I felt I needed to get away from Bethany. Most of my clientele came from the private college students, faculty, or members of the local community, and most of them were going away for the summer. I decided to take a leave of absence and agreed to return when college resumed in the fall. I called my brother Joe and asked him if the paper mill where he worked offered any type of summer employment. He called back and said I could run the chemical tests on the density of the pulp during the summer for what seemed to me to be an outrageously high salary. I informed him I would take the summer job and would be able to find a place to stay in a motel near my work.

CHAPTER SIX

My brother Joe helped me get a job for the summer of 1969 at Fiberboard Paper Mill in Antioch, California. He was a supervisor at the plant and had worked there for more than eight years. Joe warned me that many of the full-time employees saved their vacation time and any sick days they had accumulated to use for extra days off during the summer months because it was so hot working inside the mill. The high temperature in the Antioch area averaged 90 degrees during the summer. Because it was a paper mill, most of the employees had some type of direct experience with the fire furnaces, which raised the temperature in those areas of the mill by twenty to thirty percent. Some who had to work directly in the boiler area were only allowed to work fifteen-minute intervals because it was so hot in there.

My brother knew that a less physically demanding job was testing the pulp density with chemical testing. The tester ran the same chemical tests every forty-five minutes to chart and verify that the density of the board pulp was within an acceptable range. It was easy for Joe to convince me that a tester job was the best one for me. Upper level managers felt the position needed someone with at least some college experience because it required reading, charting, sample taking, retrieval of chemicals from restricted and locked cabinets, administering the test, and then verifying the test results as being within an acceptable range. If the density was not within the proper range, the entire mill was shut down and a percentage of boards that had been produced and those in the pipeline had to be re-structured or replaced. Not many mill workers were qualified to do this job, which paid substantially more than most were earning. I got the job, but I soon found out that many of my fellow testers called in sick about twice a week during the summer months. As a result of this, I averaged three days per week of my five-day work week having to work a double shift. There were three eight hour shifts each day: one from 7:00 a.m. to 3:00 p.m.; a second, 3:00 p.m. to 11:00 p.m.: and the third from 11:00 p.m. to 7:00 a.m. If you were on a shift and the person supposed to replace you called in sick, you had to continue working the entire next shift. Even though the pay for the second shift was time-and-half, most chemical specialists (what we testers were called) did not want to work an additional eight hours. It had been suggested that the person would only have to work an additional four hours and it would be up to management to find a replacement or be responsible themselves for finding a replacement for the remainder of the shift. Management did not support this suggestion. I always packed two meals just in case.

I moved to Antioch believing I could find a motel that would offer low weekly or monthly rates. Knowing how much I would earn for the three months, I felt I could afford a motel room because it fit my housing needs perfectly. The room was cleaned each day and the bed was made. When I came home from work there would be no one to distract or bother me. I only needed a place to sleep. When the front office found out I was a college student there for only the summer and would be working at the mill as a chemical specialist, they kindly lowered my room rate because I was trying to better myself.

Aunt Alma and Uncle Skip got word I was going to be in Antioch for the summer and wanted me to know that I could visit them anytime I wanted. They showed up at my room the second night I was living in the motel. I heard a knocking on my door at about 5:00 p.m. I had gotten off work at 3:00 p.m. The first week had included training and rotating shifts. My real work started the second week. Aunt Alma and Joe's wife, Jody, were good friends and Jody had told her about my moving to Antioch for the summer. I opened the door.

"Ronald, why didn't you let us know you were going to be here for three months? We would love for you to stay with us. You could save all the money this place is going to cost you," Alma said, as both she and Uncle Skip stepped into my room.

"I didn't want to bother anyone. I am going to be working every day, and Joe says many days I will work sixteen of the twenty-four hours. My plans for the summer are to sleep, eat, and work," I said.

"We have beds and plenty of food. You don't have to stay here. Your mother would want you to stay with us," she said, now sitting down on one of the two beds in my room.

"That is very nice of you, but I really want to be on my own," I said.

"You could save a lot of money if you stayed with us. Will you at least consider it?" Uncle Skip asked. I knew I did not want to change my plans. They were nice people but my twin, Donald, had given them a hard time when he lived with them and I did not want to hear about that again, nor did I want to appear to be taking advantage of them for their money or their generosity.

"It is very kind of you to offer such a proposal, but I think I am going to stay right here," I responded quickly.

"OK, but you will come to see us, won't you?" Aunt Alma asked.

"Of course," I answered. They stood up, hugged me, and left. I thought I would visit them within the next three or four weeks on one of my days off.

My in-service training ended on Friday; and my regularly scheduled shift started on Sunday. When I returned to my room on Sunday evening, I opened the door with my key and walked into a room that was cleaned from top to bottom, but none of my personal items were in the room. I immediately ran to the office, where I spotted one of the motel managers.

"How do I report a theft?" I asked.

"We have some paperwork you need to complete. Let me get it for you. You will need to put down exactly what possessions were taken," responded the manager.

"That will be simple. Every single personal possession I own was taken," I stated, trying to show the severity of what had happened to me. The manager looked down at a notebook on his side of the counter.

"Here in the notes it says, your mother came by today and moved all of your belongings home. It states that the police department was called to verify she was doing this to keep you from having to buy food, prepare lunches, and to allow you to have home cooked meals. There is a note we are supposed to give you," he said handing me an envelope with my name on the outside.

"My mother is dead. She could not have been here," I said, as I slowly turned from the counter and walked back to my room. I sat down on one of the beds and opened the envelope. The handwritten note read:

"Please forgive us for taking such a leap of faith that you will come and live with us. We have never met any young person like you. You are smart, courageous, polite, motivated, caring, and driven. You don't ask for or expect things to be given to you. If your mother were still alive, you would be her shining star. We can never replace her, but we want to be here to help guide your future if you need guiding. We will support you when you need it. We will provide direction should you ever ask. From this day forth, we want to be the parents you currently don't have. We can't replace the ones you had, but we will do our best to earn your love. Mom and Dad."

I thought for a few minutes about what they had done and what they had written in the letter. I drove to their home. They had put my belongings into a bedroom that had my name on the door. I pretended to be mad and even suggested that I might have to discuss with the police what the consequences of their breaking and entering my motel room would have made on their reputation in the community. I could not keep a straight face. I would spend the summer with them. From that day forward they never introduced me to anyone as their nephew. When it was necessary to explain our relationship to friends who knew I was not their son, they would say I was their son by another marriage. They never revealed which one of them was supposed to be my biological parent.

* * * * *

A few days later as I was about to leave for my 7:00 a.m. to 3:00 p.m. shift at Fiberboard, Mother, as I now called Aunt Alma, wanted to know what I wanted for my birthday.

"If you could have any gift you want for your birthday, what would it be?" she asked, handing me a lunchbox with two sandwiches, two bananas, chips, grapes, and a thermos of milk.

"I don't really know. You already have been so kind and are saving me so much money, please don't think you have to give me more. Let's call my living here this summer my present from you," I said.

"Think back to one of your favorite birthday parties and what kind of a gift did you like the most? Did you like clothes, or toys, or books?" she asked

"I have never had a birthday party," I admitted.

"What do you mean?" she asked, not believing anyone had not been given a birthday party in over eighteen years.

"Never had one. Now, I must leave, or I will be late for work," I said. I left without any further discussion. It was about three hours into my shift when I realized that today was my birthday. It now made sense why there had been a discussion about it earlier in the morning.

At exactly 3:00 p.m., I was relieved to see my replacement arrive. I did not want to work a double shift on my birthday. I later found out that if I had informed the company of my birthday, I would have gotten the day off with pay. No one had told me about this perk. As I drove to my new summer home, I thought I would rest in my room and thank God for all the blessings He had given me. Once I got home, I decided to shower. A distinct odor covers everyone who works at a paper mill. As I walked down the hall toward the bathroom, both of my new parents were standing in their bedroom doorway.

"Do you have any specific plans for the next few hours?" asked Mother.

"We thought it might be nice for just the three of us to go to the Riverview Lodge for dinner to honor your birthday," said Father.

"I don't have anything planned," I replied. We soon backed out of the driveway and started driving toward the restaurant. It was about seven miles away. It was on the delta and had its own boat dock and airplane landing strip. Just before we should have turned right toward the water, Father turned left.

"What is going on? I think we just turned the wrong way," I said.

"We will take you to that restaurant sometime soon, but today we want to give you your first birthday party," Mother said.

"What? When did this get planned?" I asked in disbelief.

"Today! We called some of our friends and asked if they would like to join us at the park to celebrate our son's birthday," Mother explained.

"I don't really know anyone in town yet," I said, trying to downplay what I thought might be an embarrassing turnout for them.

"We told them that you are nineteen today and that you are going to be returning to college at the end of summer. We asked them to be creative when they asked what kind of gift you might want," said Father.

"How many are you expecting?" I asked.

"We have no idea. We told them it is a surprise party, so you need to act surprised," said Mother

"I will be. Anything else I should know?" I questioned.

"We told them it is a potluck and that your favorite food is anything Mexican," Father claimed joyfully. It was his favorite type of food too!

I expected four or five people to attend. Was I surprised when we drove up to see so many cars! I could not count them all. I saw young children, teens, a few who looked to be my age, and about thirty who resembled my new parents. We had wonderful food, lots of balloons, and so many gifts we had a hard time getting them all into our station wagon. By the time I got home and into bed, I realized that I had received a great blessing that day and that I had learned a lot about love and generosity.

* * * * *

Two weeks later I received another gift, which was the best gift that ever had ever given to me by anyone. Mother and Father informed me that my sister, Sandy, was going to arrive soon for a week's visit. My sister, Helene, had taken two of my sisters, Sandy and Cathy, to live with her and her husband, Luther, when Momma died, and Father did not want to care for any of us. The four of them were going to live in Japan because Luther was being deployed there to serve for three years on an Air Force base. Helene had agreed that Sandy could visit us before they left.

Sandy and I had always been close. Many times, throughout my life it felt like we should have been twins. We had rheumatic fever at the same time. If I got sick, it would not be long before she would get sick. Sandy was now fourteen years old. I had not seen her in about a year. We drove to Stockton to the airport to pick her up. When she came down the stairs of the plane her transformation was almost indescribable. She had always been cute; now she was beautiful. Her blonde hair was really blonde, her dark suntan made most other people look pale. She was waving and smiling at me when it dawned on me that she looked like a fashion model, much older than her age.

It was the middle of that week when she told us that she did not want to move to Japan. Mother and Father called a meeting and we got on the phone with Helene and Luther. Mother and Father convinced them to allow Sandy and me to be together again. Notarized documents had to be filed and consent forms signed by all parties; but within two weeks, Mother and Father had custody of another child. Just as with me, they never introduced Sandy to anyone except as their daughter.

Every evening both Sandy and I helped at the rest home my new parents owned and operated. We would do the dishes, put out medications that did not require a licensed nurse to administer, cleaned, vacuumed, and elderly sat so that once a week Mother and Father could have a date night just for themselves.

* * * * *

Around August 1, 1969, Mother began to experience some fainting episodes. She thought it was caused by overwork. Her mother, Granny Christian, who owned a rest home with nine patients next door to ours, relied on her and Father to manage it for her, just like they took care of their own. The doctors could not determine the cause of Mother's illness. Finally, one of the specialists suggested her blood level was dropping so low it was causing her to lose consciousness. She was also retaining water and her weight was increasing noticeably. Every time she had to go to the doctor, Father, Sandy, and I went with her.

Mother read in the paper about a specialist in Tijuana, who was supposed to be using new techniques that had not been approved for use in the United States but were gaining much attention. He was also using medications in his clinic that were not approved by our Food and Drug Administration. We loaded ourselves into the station wagon and drove from Antioch to Tijuana to see if he could offer a cure for Mother. Unfortunately, we determined his operation was a scam and we did not return.

The time for me to go back to Bethany arrived. We packed my Mustang and their station wagon, and our new family went with me back to the campus. They left me on Sunday around noon. I checked in with them Sunday evening about seven and thanked them for helping me move back to the dorms. We all said goodnight.

The next morning at about 9:00 a.m., the dorm resident knocked on my door and handed me a piece of paper with a phone number on it and said he was told it was an emergency and that I should call this number. I immediately went to the pay phone at the end of our hall. I dialed the number although I did not recognize it.

"Dr. Bellham speaking, how may I help you?" answered Mother's personal physician.

"This is Ron Reel. I was told I needed to call this number as soon as possible," I stated.

"Yes, I have been trying to get hold of you. Your mother was admitted to the hospital early this morning. She is not in very good condition and we are doing our best to stabilize her. When I asked where you were, because it was the first time you were not here when I had to treat her, they told me you were back at college and not to disturb you," he said. As he ended his sentence I interrupted.

"Should I leave now and come directly to the hospital?" I asked.

"That is entirely up to you. Not only is she worried about her own condition, she is now worrying about your being away from home," he said.

"What would you do?" I asked the doctor.

"If I loved your mother as much as I think you do, I would come as quickly as possible. I would put my studies on hold or find a local college that would allow me to complete my general education courses and be home and near her. But, again, I am not you," he said.

Dr. Bellham, do not tell my family we had this conversation. I can get my college degree from many different places. I do not want to lose Mother or be a cause of her stress. Been there, done that, don't want to do it again," I said.

When I finished the call, I went back to my dorm room and started packing my belongings. What I could not fit into my car, I gave to other students who could use them.

It was late afternoon when I arrived back home and drove to the hospital. Mother was in bed; Father was on one side holding her hand; Sandy was on the other side holding that hand. When I stood at the end of her bed, Father and Sandy took my hands and we were a united family, ready to face the world.

Happily, Mother was out of the hospital within a week. In a few weeks Dr. Bellham located the exact cause of her blackouts and with the correct medicine and treatments, she stabilized and was able to recognize the symptoms before they happened and was able to take appropriate action.

* * * *

I enrolled at San Joaquin Delta College (SJD), about twenty miles from our home because Father and Mother thought it was an outstanding community college with very inexpensive tuition and, besides, Father had attended there. They also felt that because it was next door to the University of the Pacific, a very well-respected private university, where I might transfer for my last two years, allowing me to remain at home even longer. They liked the idea that Delta was close enough that I could come home after classes each day.

I started community college and Sandy started high school during the same week. We both wanted to help more with the rest home. Father and Mother suggested we become licensed nurses' assistants. We enrolled in a class at Tracy Memorial Hospital that met once each week. They offered a credentialed and certified program. Tracy was only about twenty miles south of our home, and it was almost all freeway driving.

Father and Mother were impressed that I always opened the car door for any woman or girl. Father claimed that was a sign of a polite gentleman. One November evening I had gotten home from Delta just in time for us to get to our 7:00 p.m. class in Tracy. I had been up late the last few nights studying, preparing speeches, practicing lines for the play I was in, and working in the rest home.

By the time we got home, I felt it a miracle not to have had an auto accident. I turned the engine off, got out of the car, stumbled into the house, went to my bedroom, and did not even get into my pajamas; I just crashed. I was awakened by a knocking on my door.

"Ronald, Ronald, are you OK?" I heard Mother asking.

"Just tired, I will be fine. What time is it?" I asked.

"About 10:45 p.m. Do you know where your sister is?" she asked. Class was over at 9:00 p.m. It had taken us about twenty minutes to get home.

"Isn't she in her room?" I asked.

"No! Where could she be?" asked Mother, sounding worried. I quickly retraced my actions from the time I parked the car.

"Oh, my God," I said pushing myself from my bed and moving my body toward the door. I continued, "I bet I know where she is," I said, opening my bedroom door, stumbling through the living room, and rushing out the front door. Mother followed me. Sandy was sitting in the passenger seat of my car. I went over and opened her door for her.

"I knew you would be back because gentlemen always open doors for women," she said laughing, smiling, and trying to make this a moment we would never forget. She succeeded. We have laughed many times about the ultimate test I had taken and almost failed.

CHAPTER SEVEN

By the end of my first week at San Joaquin Delta College, I had adjusted to the drive from Antioch to Stockton, settled into eighteen unit's worth of courses, and was thinking of joining the choir, the theatre department, and/or the competitive speech team called forensics.

Mother and Father had gone to school with Dallas, the owner of the Chevron gas station in our town. They were close friends. Although they did not have a Chevron credit card, they had an account, which allowed them to charge services and gasoline for a month and then pay for what they had spent at the end of the month. Dallas was told to allow me to have my car serviced and to let me fill my car with gas when I needed it, just another example of my parents' generosity. I had gotten gas on Wednesday when Dallas himself waited on me. There was a sign in the station window seeking hourly help. I informed him I didn't like working on cars, but I could pump gas. He told me he was seeking someone to simply pump gas. Because of his friendship with the Nortons, he offered to hire me for ten hours per week.

That evening when I got home from school, I shared with the family my conversation with Dallas: "When I got gas this morning, I noticed a sign in the window for a part-time job at the station," I said.

"Dallas is a nice person and I am sure he would be easy to work for in that type of work. He tries to give local high school boys an opportunity to learn a trade and help with the financial obligations of struggling families," explained Mother.

"I think he tries them out for a few months, pumping gas only. If they make it through the trial stage, he begins to expand their training to lead them into a trade they will have for life," continued Father.

"It seems like he is having a positive impact on the town," I said.

"Yes! Especially for young men not smart enough to go to college," Mother agreed.

"I am sure the owner of a gas station makes more than some people who have a bachelor's degree," I shared.

"When he was living with us, we tried to get your brother Donald to work for Dallas," added Father, "but it did not work out."

"How did your day at college go?" asked Mother, trying to change the subject.

"It was fine. I just have one more thing to say about Dallas. He offered me a job today," I said proudly.

"Why would he offer you a job?" Mother asked.

"He probably thought a bright young person, like you, could do a good job for him," Father said, trying to clarify what happened.

"No. I asked him for a job, and he said he will hire me," I said somewhat conceitedly.

"But why would you want to work there?" Mother wanted to know.

"So, I can help with all the costs I am going to have driving back and forth to Stockton, my tuition, my books, food, and most importantly, entertainment," I said smiling.

"But for the next few years college will be your job. We want you to see that as your sole job; except for helping us out from time to time with senior sitting so we can go on dates," Mother said.

"We are in a financial position that does not require you to have any job except college, if you live at home. We will be responsible for all your expenses," added Father.

"I don't think that is fair to you or me. From time to time I may want extra spending money or pick up a gift for someone, or...you see my drift, right?" I said, protesting what they were suggesting.

"We will give you $100 per month to use any way you want. You will have no accountability to us for that money. We want your college to be your only job. What do you say?" Father asked.

"I still think I should help pay my own way," I said.

"Doing well in college, participating in extracurricular activities, and studying, all are integral parts of your education," Father explained.

"Let's try it our way for one semester. In January, we can convene again and evaluate if we want to make any adjustments. Are you willing to agree to those terms?" asked Mother. They both paused and waited for my response.

"I think I must be dreaming. You want me to have no job except to go to college and have fun?" I teased.

"We do expect good grades," Mother added.

"I can live up to that without a doubt," I confirmed.

"Let's shake hands and then you go call Dallas and tell him you won't need to take him up on his generous offer," said Father.

I returned to SJD on Monday, trying to decide between being a music major with a minor in drama, or drama major with a minor in music. During my acting class, two guys were talking about a newly hired thirty-year old professor, who according to them, was as hot as any woman could be.

"This professor could be a beauty pageant winner," one declared.

"If you walk down the hall or around the campus with her, the other men on campus will think she is your date and be jealous," avowed the other boy. "Not only is she attractive, she is teaching competitive speech as a class and needs two more students in order for the class to make," he continued in a pleading voice.

"I did some competitive speech in high school," I said, smiling shyly.

"As soon as this class is over, let's go see her. I think her office hour is about the time this class lets out," the first boy said. During the rest of my drama class, all I could do was to think about how I might join her class and add some additional units to the eighteen I already was carrying.

When class ended, the three of us marched over to her office where we were surprised to see three other male students leaving with add slips. She stood and acknowledged us. She informed us she was headed toward her class and asked us if we wanted to walk with her. We arrived at her classroom and took a seat.

"Hello to those already registered in this class. I see you have brought some additional people with you today. I hope you all will be interested in enrolling in this speech class, which will develop your self-worth and help you deliver speeches in public in a dynamic and professional way. Do any of you remember what we talked about during our last class?" she asked.

"You told us to not be afraid of asking for help when we are selecting topics and that you would help us learn how to move across a stage when speaking at certain types of gatherings," said one of the students.

"You also told us we are going to learn how to construct a variety of different types of speeches," added one of the girls in the class.

"Mrs. Vogler, do you now have enough students for this class to make?" asked another student.

"Currently we do, but if any of you drop, we won't. I am hoping we get at least two more students than we need," she clarified.

"I would like to join, but I currently have eighteen units and don't know if the administration will allow me to take any additional units," I said.

"You must be a good student for the administration to allow you to be at that level. I can go see a counselor if you need assistance. Have you done any speech competition before?" she asked, looking only at me.

"I did dramatic interpretation and Lions Club speaking in high school. I am considering being a drama major," I shared.

"That is just what we need, more actors!" said a slightly round, if not pudgy, boy. Mrs. Vogler ignored the comment.

"I would consider it an honor to have you join us," she said, looking again in my direction.

"I would consider it an honor to be coached by you. Do you have an add slip for me?" I asked.

"I happen to have a couple," she said, with a smile. The class was scheduled for Tuesday and Thursday from 11:00 a.m. until 12:30 p.m. From my perspective, it was tantalizing to watch her, to see her move, to observe her facial expressions, to hear her voice, and to have her smile at me. I was surprised that her class was in danger of being cancelled for low enrollment. It had to be that not enough males knew about her. By the next meeting there were over thirty students registered in the class: twenty-seven males and five females.

Mrs. Vogler previewed the various competitive events. She then asked each of us to select two different events in which we wanted to participate. I chose oral interpretation of literature (reading a published work of literature) and persuasive speaking (creating my own persuasive message). The only event she had no volunteers for was debate. When she explained the amount of time and dedication, practice, and research needed, I felt it would be too much for me. Two weeks later, she shared with us that two of her student debaters from the high school where she had taught the previous year were enrolling late and would be our debate team. At this same time, she shared with us some very personal information; she was in the final stages of a divorce from her husband. She said he was a teacher at the high school where she had taught, and that they had a five-year-old child, but he would have primary custody of her. The entire class felt badly for her situation; but some of the young men, including myself, were inwardly hoping she might someday find us attractive.

When Mr. Rudee, an esteemed visiting professor from UC Berkeley, found out that many of his actors were now committed to the speech program in general, and forensics, in particular, he went out of his way to try to convince us to choose drama over forensics.

"I hear that some of you are trying to be both actors and public speakers. Both are worthy activities. Each will need total concentration, rehearsal time, skill, and dedication. I don't know of a single person who has been able to master both at the same time. One will always take a second seat. I hear we have hired a young, energetic, talented, and quite nice-looking forensics director. That program is in its infancy. Our theatre program is one of the most highly recognized programs around; that is why I am in residency this year. Our stage, lighting, and the seats in our auditorium are state-of-the-art. Millions of dollars have been spent to ensure your training on this stage will have you ready for transfer to the best drama department at the university level or go directly into professional theatres across the country. Our speech team doesn't even have a budget yet. It is my understanding that students may have to pay to participate. I am sure with her previous forensics successes; it won't take long for her to convince the college to provide a budget.

"Well, enough said. You are welcome to try both; but if you are one of our top actors, you may have to make a choice because many of the weekends have conflicts of scheduled performances between us and speech competitions," he lectured his captive audience. None of the three of us who had joined forensics wanted or auditioned for a major role in that semester's production of "Romeo and Juliet." In fact, the title role went to a student from another nearby community college, while several other major roles were given to University of the Pacific students.

Our first assignment in the drama class was to create a face from paper mache. This assignment was supposed to teach us how to examine various aspects of the face because it is the most expressive part of the body. Father was a master creator and inventor. When I shared this assignment with the family, it was he who suggested we take one of Mother's mannequin heads and paper mache it. He helped me with the construction of the molding and adhering the strips in each direction around the face of the mannequin until the full face was ready for coloring. We took liquid make-up and applied it in different shades at various places on the face. We used lighter shades around the nose, darker on the chin; the combined colors blended into a seamless composite. We then took powdered make-up from Mother's own personal make-up collection. We used her false eye lashes and lipstick to help color the cheeks and to accent the lips. I styled one of her wigs and the project was complete. I always bragged that Father and I earned a grade of "A+" when we worked as a team.

On the speech side of classwork, Mrs. Vogler had each of us sign-up to spend thirty-minute individual coaching sessions with her when she was not teaching in class. She posted a sign-up sheet outside her office and you chose when you wanted to have your individual appointment to practice one-on-one with her. It was challenging to find out she tailored your meetings specifically for you. She gave you specific assignments. If you returned and had not completed your assignment, she would end your session immediately and send you off to the library or to someplace you needed to go to complete what she had instructed you to do during your last session with her.

My oral interpretation was progressing nicely. We were working on the development of voices, learning to emphasize certain words, establish cadence, help with the "mountain and valleys" of storytelling, as she called them. Every storyteller needs highly intense moments as well as slow and thoughtful reflective moments. Too long in any one area results in a loss of audience attention.

My persuasive speech was more of a struggle. We had narrowed my topic selection to three topics. In our session today, we were to decide on the topic I would use for competition for the year. She told me there would be many revisions made, and each revision would make it better than before.

"You have done everything I have asked, Ron. You have done research on each topic; you have divided what you think are three logical aspects for development. Now it is time for you to choose the one topic you think your audience will want to learn the most about, feel the deepest, and be willing to act upon an acceptable solution step. Don't forget, Aristotle told us to always remember the audience when we are preparing a speech. We need to tailor our message to them, so we need to understand where they are at each step of our journey. Are you ready to declare your final topic?" she asked.

"I am ready. It was a difficult decision, but I have chosen to write my speech on what we can do to stop child abuse in America," I said.

"Why did you choose that topic?" she asked.

"Because many children cannot speak-up for themselves," I shared.

"Any other reason?" she asked.

"I was abused as a child and no one spoke up for me when it was happening. I want to be the voice for all children who cannot speak out," I said, barely able to hold back tears. I could see Mrs. Vogler's eyes filling with tears as well.

"That is beautifully stated. Just a caution, sometimes certain topics are so close to us that we get too emotional when talking about them. If we get in the way of our message because of our emotions, the audience will feel sorry for us instead of feeling empathy for the subjects of our topic," she shared, as she reached over and took my hand for a short moment. I could tell she was concerned for abused children.

"I think I have made the right choice," I said.

"You may be the first male student to talk on this topic at the college level. Most men don't share their feelings and that fact will need to be shown tastefully. Your assignment for our next meeting is to choose your three main points of development and I will see you next week. Our first contest is in three weeks. We will get the body of your speech done next week, the introduction and conclusion the following week, and the week before the contest, I want you to give your speech before as many beginning public speaking classes as you can. Is that understood?" she asked, rising from her desk and escorting me to the door of her office.

Our first contest was at the University of the Pacific (UOP). It was a Friday, Saturday, and Sunday affair. There was one round of each of my two events on Friday. Saturday had two more rounds which completed what were called the preliminary rounds. I made it to the semi-final round in both events on Saturday as well. The final rounds for all the events were scheduled for Sunday.

I drove home Saturday feeling proud of myself, my team, and my coach. Saturday night my family asked how I had done in the contest. Once I told them of the results they wanted to know if I objected to them coming to my final rounds on Sunday. It was a far cry from my experiences in high school when none of my family wanted to see me perform.

"Where can we meet you tomorrow and what time should we be at the college?" asked Mother.

"We are so proud. Remember, you have already been chosen as one of the top seven students in two different events," added Father.

"As you enter the university, you will see signs directing you to the posting area. Arrive at 10:30 a.m. I will be looking for you. By arriving at that time, you will have plenty of time to get to the room where I will be speaking. Are you sure you want to come? You don't have to be there. If you choose not to show up, I won't be angry," I said, hoping they would quickly respond how much it meant for them to attend. There was a long pause.

"We don't want to be anyplace else tomorrow," insisted Mother

"I will make sure they are ready on time. I want us to get there early enough to get front row seats," said Father.

"If you don't mind, it might be better this first time if you sit midway or even toward the back of the room. You can be my own critique team, informing me about my volume and movements," I declared.

"Whatever you want," said Sandy. She continued, "This will be my first time to see you compete too!" she said, as she jumped up and hugged me.

I got mixed reactions from some of my teammates when I shared the fact that my family would be watching my final rounds. Some thought it was a good idea, but others thought it would make me feel nervous; some feared they would be a distraction. I, however, was ecstatic. I had wanted family support for my speaking engagements ever since I could remember.

Sandy and our parents showed up for both rounds. They did clap a little longer after my performances than the rest of the audience. I heard them say after the round was over and people were leaving the room that I was their son and they thought I should win. After we got home, I thanked them for attending and for supporting me. I then explained that it was proper protocol for them to let others know that I was their son, but not to say that I should win because some of the other participants might feel such statements were designed to influence the judges and we had to allow the judges to make up their own minds.

"Well, hells bells, of course we wanted to influence the judges. People need to know when you speak you are the best," Father said in a very boastful and loud voice.

"We will scream it out, but only in our minds, in the future," promised Mother.

I thought they were correct about my being the best, but the judges felt I earned second place in oral interpretation and third in persuasive speaking. My entire family was pleased by my accomplishment.

* * * * *

Each week my meeting with Coach Vogler made both of my programs stronger and more competitive. She had a way of praising you and then forcing you to see weaknesses and propose ways to fix those problems. An example was our meeting the week following the UOP tournament. We read through the judges' comment cards together.

"The comments are full of praise for your topic. The judges all loved your speaking style and showmanship. You won on your delivery. The judges want more content, better emotional examples, and a cleaner and simpler action step. What do you think might be a sentence or two we could insert to make crystal clear what you want the listeners to do after they recognize that a serious problem exists?"

"I don't think they hear these children crying out and many of the judges are not willing to listen because they don't identify with such horrific treatment," I responded. Coach thought for a few seconds and then wrote something in the notebook she used for writing information at the meetings she would give you at the end of the session.

"Why not ask directly, 'Do you hear the children weeping?' as the thematic developer and transition opening from one major point to the next?" she asked. Every week, with the revisions, my speech kept getting better.

Meanwhile it was about time for "Romeo and Juliet" to open. I had a small role which I felt offered a central plot change in projecting the message of the play. I kidded myself. I had fourteen lines. Mr. Rudee expected all of us to be at every evening rehearsal. The play was sold out for each performance. I questioned not using Delta's students in all the major roles because I thought we would learn more. The director felt we were learning from the almost professional students who worked with us and set examples for us to emulate. I guess both worked to some degree. Without the ringers, our productions would not have been as good and the sold-out ticket sales might not have occurred.

The last performance had certain traditional elements. We were informed it was called a rap party, taking place right after the final curtain came down that night. The entire cast and staff stayed after the show and broke down the stage, put the drops away, and replaced the flats and platforms, furniture, and props in the warehouse located just off the stage. All clothing was returned to the costume department located on the other side of the stage. When we left the stage that night, it was perfectly bare.

*　*　*　*　*

One of the highlights for us newbies was called the cast party. It was being held a few nights later at a cast member's personal residence. We were given directions to the site the last night of the play's performance. I had no idea who was responsible for coordinating the event. We were told there would be food, drinks, and lots of loving each other for a job well done.

Some of the cast members carpooled to the party. I took my Mustang because my plans were to be seen, have something to eat, celebrate the successful run, compliment those actors deserving of such praise, and then skip out and return home. The statement about plenty of food, drinks, and love were accurate. I figured there would be food and drink. What surprised me was the outright displays of affection people were displaying toward each other. People who had not spoken to each other during the play now were hugging and kissing each other. Another shock for me was the smell of marijuana that permeated certain parts of the house. Within ten minutes of arriving, I was asked if I wanted to partake. I politely declined several times.

I noticed two cast members sitting together in the corner of the formal living room. They too were minor characters in the play. We had smiled and chit-chatted a couple of times during the rehearsals and after the performances. One of them signaled for me to come to where they were sitting. As I made my way toward them, someone handed me a glass of what I thought was wine. Both girls were smiling now that I was moving toward them. I put down the glass before arriving at the sofa.

"Quite some party, don't you think?" the blonde said. She quickly looked at her friend and giggled. Before I could answer her, her friend spoke, "We both think you are cute and much nicer than most of the other guys in the show," she said, punching her friend's shoulder. Both girls giggled at the same time.

"I must say you have made an accurate assessment of me. I plead guilty to being a nice guy; but this nice guy doesn't even know your names," I said.

"I am Rebecca, and this is my friend and roommate Cherry," said the blonde. I extended my hand to meet and greet them by shaking hands.

Cherry had dark hair and she looked very exotic. I thought she might be Greek or Armenian.

"I am Ron; it is nice to finally meet both of you officially. Do you mind if I join you?" I asked.

"We invited you to join us," said Cherry, as she scooted away from Rebecca, so I had room to sit between them.

"Did you enjoy being in the play?" I asked, leaving it vague enough for either or both to answer.

"This is our third production. We like the social aspect and the parties these people throw. Quite a few of the main characters have parties throughout the productions. Once they get to know you, they invite you to those parties that are in addition to the final cast party.

"These big cast parties provide an outlet for us to show a lot of affection toward each other," said Rebecca.

"Do you want to express affection tonight?" I asked.

"We have been with almost all of the straight guys before. Each show finds more straight guys. We are just two horny all-American girls," said Cherry, as she placed her hand on my lap.

"Are you straight or will our conversation just be pleasant with no sexual gratification?" asked Rebecca, who kissed one of her fingers and touched my lips.

"I have never had sex with a male if that is what you are asking," I said, sitting back and pushing my body to the backside of the sofa. These few words appeared to be magical to the two of them. Suddenly a girl, who was standing in front of us, offered a tray of glasses full of beverages.

"These are full of punch; non-alcoholic drinks for those of us who have to drive home some time tonight or in the morning," she said, handing each of us a glass. We would see her several more times during the next half hour. We toasted each other. Our conversation appeared to be about discovering likes and dislikes, but each statement ended with a sexual innuendo. I was experiencing some internal changes within my body. It felt warm; I felt very happy as if I suddenly loved everything and everybody.

"Rebecca's boyfriend couldn't be here tonight," said Cherry.

"Actually, I didn't tell him about the party. He thinks the show ends next weekend. I will have to tell him I got confused," she shared, now leaning toward me offering an opportunity to kiss her. Cherry appeared to be her accomplice by directing my body with a slight push toward her as she began massaging my shoulders. Rebecca would kiss me and then turn me toward Cherry. I was being used as a tennis ball, served back and forth between the two. From time to time more punch would appear. I began paying special attention to the bass sounds of the music being played throughout the house. Lamps and other lights suddenly had multiple colors and rings around the outer parts of objects. Both of my new friends looked as though they were glowing.

"Are you ready to leave?" asked Cherry.

"Do you want to go home with us, or do you have a place where we all can stay?" asked Rebecca.

"I live with my parents. How far away is your place?" I asked.

"Not far. About ten minutes. Do you think you can drive? You can follow us, or you can ride with us and we will bring you back to get your car tomorrow," said Cherry. I felt uneasy and different, but I did not know or trust that they were in a better state of mind than I was.

"I will follow you," I said, rising from the sofa where we had been the entire time. I was suddenly taking deep breaths, focusing on walking without weaving, and trying to convince myself I was still in control. We arrived at their car first. I was parked about ten cars down from them. I should never have gotten behind the wheel of my vehicle. I was not fit to drive.

I followed them to their small house and parked on the street. We all walked, stumbled, and held on to each other until we were in the house.

The girls led me into one of the bedrooms, where there was lots of kissing and rubbing. Our clothes were still on. Suddenly there was a loud knock on the front door, and we heard a male voice.

"Becky, Rebecca are you home? Come and let me in. I got off work early," called out Rebecca's boyfriend. She left to go to the living room. On her way out she slammed the bedroom door. It was now just Cherry and I; I was still a virgin. I didn't think that would be the case for long. Cherry was unbuttoning my shirt and was taking her blouse off when the bedroom door opened, and Rebecca said in a loud voice, "Jeremy wants us to party together. Can we do a four-way?" she asked. I did not know for sure what that meant. I thought I did not want to be a part of whatever it was.

"Sure, that OK with me," said Cherry.

"I don't think so," was all I could utter.

"OK, see yourself out and we hope to see you at another party soon," said Cherry. Both girls and Jeremy left me on the bed, and I heard the three of them making lots of noise next door. I redressed myself and left. Once I got to my car, I knew I was still impaired. I felt I needed to take a nap. I closed my eyes and woke up around 3:00 a.m. I felt better and thought if I concentrated on my driving, I could get home safely. I was lucky I did not run into any other car. The lights of approaching vehicles seemed bright and fuzzy. I was fortunate I did not run off the road into the river running next to it, which is still claiming lives today. I was lucky that my parents were spending the night at Granny Christian's rest home and did not know when I arrived home. God had watched over me again.

I woke up about 9:00 a.m. The drapes in my bedroom usually prevented sunshine when I did not want it. I had not closed the drapes. As I awakened, I seemed to be drawn to the warmth of the sun. I felt I needed to feel the sun's rays, providing me the energy I craved.

Father had created a comfortable sitting area at the east end of our home. It was complete with a koi pond with waterfall cascading into the fishpond to keep the water oxygenated for the fish. He had many various sized pots full of different colored flowers, plants, and even special trees. The sitting arrangement included swings, chairs, and tables. One could easily feel this area was like the Garden of Eden.

I was basking in the sunshine in one of the lounge chairs. I had placed it in a reclining position and was lying on my back so I could experience the sun's rays, which were calling to me. Father approached.

"Son, you don't usually sunbathe. Is something the matter?" he asked me.

"I know, but I have this urge, an almost uncontrollable need to feel the sunshine on my body. I feel like I must connect with the warm rays. Before you came in, I felt like I was transporting myself toward the sun. I was having an out-of-body experience," I said, trying to explain my condition.

"Did you get drunk or high last night?" Father asked calmly and caringly.

"I limited myself to regular punch," I shared.

"It appears to me someone might have spiked the punch. Did you experience any strange body or mind alterations?" asked Father.

"You won't be mad?" I asked hopefully.

"You made it home safely, which is the most important consideration. It sounds to me like some person wanted those of you drinking punch to get high for some reason," he suggested.

"The music sounded different. The bass was very loud, and my body felt like moving to the beat as I heard the music. All the colored items had a psychedelic color scheme. People appeared to have a ring of light surrounding their bodies," I shared.

"Sounds like someone put LSD in the punch," Father said calmly but emphatically.

"What makes you think that?" I asked.

"Your condition and your responses. Let's not tell your Mother. If you feel you need to bask in the sun, go to the backside of the house where no one will see you," he suggested.

Father never passed judgment. He was always steady, calm, and collected.

"Promise you won't tell Mother. I wouldn't want to let her down," I pleaded as I got up from the lounge chair.

"This is just between us. Remember I too was young once," he pointed out. Around noon I no longer needed to be attached to the sun. I found out on Monday that several people had been severely injured in car accidents, arguments between fellow actors had taken place, and physical fights had ensued. Some of the students thought the punch made them paranoid, while others felt they could conquer any task or dare. The entire week was spent trying to figure out who had tampered with the punch. No guilty party was ever determined.

CHAPTER EIGHT

As I was finishing my English class on Wednesday, my professor, Mrs. Dodgen, asked me to stay for a minute after class. I felt honored that she wanted to talk with me. Perhaps she wanted to provide direction or offer some assistance with the last paper I had turned into her. It was the written version of my persuasive speech. I even thought she might ask me to help tutor some of the students who were not as motivated as I or who found it difficult to write cogently.

"Thanks for staying after class. I want to begin by assuring you I have spent much time deciding how to approach this moment. I like you as a person and think you have something to offer to society in the future, but we all must learn to follow rules and you have violated a very serious one. I cannot let you get away with plagiarism. You turned in someone else's work as your own and that is a violation that cannot be tolerated," she said, looking directly at me. I did not know what to say. I had never copied any of my work. I thought for just a minute she was pretending to be angry because she had spent a lot time lecturing us about how to cite sources correctly, and I had done that.

"Mrs. Dodgen, I assure you, you are mistaken," I said. "I have never plagiarized anything."

"I think you intentionally took something you read by a scholar who has similar views to those you discuss in your essay. For some reason you turned his scholarly paper into me, expecting it to be so good that I would have no choice but to accept it. I have not found the actual writer yet; but I am trying to discover the sources of this paper," she said in an aggressive manner.

"I promise you the paper is mine. You won't find it anywhere else because it is mine," I insisted.

"You have two choices and I am agreeable to either. Do the last assignment over, knowing the highest grade I will give you will be a "D" grade; or drop the class and take it over again next semester with another professor. I should take this matter to the dean and have you expelled from this college. Should you challenge me, I will seek your expulsion and will try to have you barred from all public colleges in California."

"But I did not cheat," I repeated as I fought back the tears.

"The writing is too skilled, and the vocabulary and choice of words are above your level or that of any student attending this junior college," she declared.

"We have never talked in person before. What makes you think you know me, know my schooling, or know about my training. I thought you were going to make suggestions on how I could make it even better.

"This writing is so sophisticated that it cannot be your own work. You will be a better person if you don't pass off the work of a scholar as your own," she said, while retreating behind the desk to retrieve her purse. I must go to another class right now, but I will give you twenty-four hours to admit your mistake. If you do not do so, I will begin the process of having you dismissed from this school," she said as she left the room.

I didn't know what to do. I literally ran all the way to Mrs. Vogler's office to ask her for help. Luckily, I found her in her office. As I entered, she said, "Hi, Ron, what's the matter? You look like you've been crying. Please sit down."

I did but had too much energy to stay put. I stood again. "You won't believe what just happened to me," I told her. "I had to write a persuasive essay for my English teacher, Mrs. Dodgen, and I wrote a slightly revised version of my persuasive speech. She says I have plagiarized it because it is written at a level above that of most of the students at San Joaquin Delta College. She says that if I do not admit what I have done and apologize for it, she will have me thrown out of school and barred from enrolling at any public college in California. She can't do that, can she?"

"Of course not. She is just trying to frighten you into admitting you did something you did not do. I will call the English department office and make an appointment to see her before she leaves the campus this afternoon. Before I do that, however, I need some information from you. I know you started working with this subject matter late in August, how many drafts do you think you have done?"

"At least a dozen or more," I responded.

"You talked with a number of faculty members on this campus about your paper. Please give me their names and the names of their departments."

I wrote the names down and gave her the list.

"Am I right in thinking you would prefer not to remain in Mrs. Dodgen's class?"

"Oh yes. She thinks my paper is so sophisticated that it cannot be my own work. I think she gives all teachers a bad name. If she can't appreciate or be glad for someone like me who has overcome where I once was to be where I am now, she needs to reevaluate the work of all the students here. Just because we attend a junior college and not the University of California does not mean we are dumb or less motivated than anyone else," I told her. "My new class needs to be at the same time and on the same days as her class was. You know my schedule is already quite full."

"That is all the information I need," she said. "Go home and don't worry. I will take care of this as soon she is available."

When I returned home, Mother informed me that the chair of the English Department had called and wanted me to know that because of the high level of my writing, I was being moved into a more challenging English class with other outstanding writers. I decided not to tell my mother about my run-in with Mrs. Dodgen.

A few teachers along my educational journey prejudged or stereotyped me because of my background. Thank God, other incredible and life changing teachers, like Ginger Vogler, trusted their own abilities to help transform my life so that someday I would be able to help my students find the strength and courage to move forward into whatever career they wanted.

* * * * *

At every tournament SJD attended, more students were earning awards. Most awards were earned by males because we outnumbered the females this first semester of intercollegiate competition. Some of our college competitors had given us a nickname, which we proudly accepted. We were honored to be branded as "Ginger's disciples."

All the hard work done by those of us selected to attend the Western States speech contest appeared to have paid off. Twelve males and four females would represent SJD. Because Coach Vogler was always dressed so professionally and her hair always styled perfectly, some of the guys kidded her that if and when we won a major sweepstakes, they were going to celebrate by throwing her into a pool or drenching her with Gatorade, like winning athletes do at sports events.

All sixteen of us advanced to the elimination rounds. Coach called us together for a meeting in the lobby of the hotel where we were staying. "I just want all of you to know how excited and proud I am today. It is an honor to call you my students. We have worked hard this semester and you have exceeded my expectations. Go to bed and dream about how successful each of you will be tomorrow," she said, motioning for us to go to our rooms. As we began retreating, we had to pass close to the swimming pool. One of the boys shouted that it was time to do what we had been threatening to do all semester.

"Ginger Vogler, SJD coach extraordinaire, you have taken us from slightly talented novices and molded us into your image of class, dedication, and respectability," he said.

"That means a lot to me. Now get to bed," Coach Vogler commanded. Instead, some of the boys moved closer toward her.

"It is now the time we have told you would come because of our success and your coaching," a senior competitor declared. He motioned and six of our male students (three on each side of her) picked her up and carried her to the pool. They counted down from five to one and then threw her into the water. She had been protesting but to no avail. As she got out of the pool her clothes wet, and her usually beautifully styled hair was soaked and clinging to her face. She was totally drenched.

"You are all going to be paid back. You owe me big time. Go to your rooms," she shouted to all of us. I did, but about twenty minutes later I left my room and walked across the street to a drug store and bought some hair color to use for Coach Vogler. I knocked on her door.

"Mrs. Vogler, it's Ron, may I see you please?" I asked.

"Not now. Can't it wait? I am trying to make myself presentable for tomorrow. I can fix everything except my hair. I don't have much talent in that department," she said in a desperate and down-trodden manner behind the closed door.

"If you open the door, I promise you that I have a secret and a talent to share that will make your day," I said, trying to bait her into letting me in.

"Unless you are a fantastic hair stylist, who knows how to color my once blond bleached hair that is now green from the chlorine in the pool, I don't think you can help," she responded.

"This is your lucky night. I can make you look exactly like you did before you were thrown into the pool," I said confidently. The door slowly opened and revealed her in pajamas with her wet hair streaming down onto her face.

"Look at me, I don't think you can help me. I can't help myself," she said, opening the door and revealing her complete devastation.

"You do know that throwing you in the pool was a gesture of love, don't you? I am going to tell you something that I have not shared with anyone else at this college. I am a licensed cosmetologist. I have taken a hiatus from work to concentrate on school. If you allow me help you, I brought with me a product from Loreal named, 'Platinum Blonde 101,' and we can make sure that not one person tomorrow will know anything happened to you or to your hair tonight," I promised. Just the hope of rescuing her seemed to ease her apprehension.

"Let me see what you brought with you," she said, smiling and putting on a brave face.

"I brought color, curling iron, blower, my special styling comb, and lots of hairspray. I can put you back together," I promised. After about an hour Coach Vogler's hair looked almost identical to how it usually appeared. Not to brag, but my style was softer around her cheekbones and I had raised the height of the top of her hair a smidgen. She was amazed.

"You cannot tell anyone who did this for you. I don't want to become the SJD hair stylist," I said. She thought about her answer.

"This can be our secret under one condition. If I need refreshing at any tournament, I can call on you," she suggested.

The next morning, no one could figure out how she looked so perfect. She always told us how she didn't do hair and that her stylist was the only one who ever touched her hair. Mrs. Vogler said she had made a desperate call and her stylist had made a midnight special visit. I took that statement as a very high compliment. Only our squad knew about the pool incident and Coach Vogler's unexpected plunge. It was quite thrilling to see her looking so perfect as she made sure we all knew where to go to do battle. As a team, we placed third in overall sweepstakes and first among community colleges. I placed second in oral interpretation and first in persuasion.

CHAPTER NINE

My biological father, whom my new family now called "Uncle Bill," had shown up unexpectedly in Antioch about six weeks before our last tournament. I could not stand to be in his presence. I had done my best to forgive him for abandoning us and for not staying committed to Momma or to their wedding vows, but I did not like him. Mother and Father Norton, however, were insisting that Sandy and I renew our relationship with him. My new mother had spent many summer months with our family when she was growing up. She and my oldest sister, Nellie, were the same age. We had been told Alma was my father's stepbrother's first wife's child. She was more like a second cousin. Our parents told us to call her Aunt Alma.

When Uncle Bill, as I now called my biological father, showed up, he skillfully used his acting ability even better than he had immediately after Momma's funeral. He was sitting at the dining room table when I arrived home from college.

"Look who just showed up today!" Mother shouted gleefully. I had not looked at anyone seated at the table. Someone was always visiting. I looked and my stomach felt sick.

"Aren't you going to say hello to your father?" she asked, moving toward him. I did not want to respond. I had nothing to say to him.

"Imagine, you and me both staying with Alma," he said. I could not imagine any scenario in which I would allow this to happen.

"I see you have a guest. I hope you enjoy his visit. I have to go study," I said and I went directly to my bedroom.

"Ronald, ain't ya gonna say somethin' to me?" he asked as I continued to walk away from him while I answered, "I think we have said enough to each other for a lifetime."

"Well, I guess you'll have to warm up to the fact that we both gonna be living together again," he said, standing and moving toward the front door. I assumed he was going out to have a cigarette. It was only a minute or two when I heard a knock at my bedroom door.

"Ron, honey, can we talk?" asked mother.

"I really have to study. Can it wait?" I responded.

"Don't be mad, but Uncle Bill just showed up," she shared.

"I know you have good memories about him and Momma. If you want him here, that is up to you. I don't want him near me," I said, moving to open the door.

"I realize you are upset," she said as I opened the door.

"We both cannot live here. I just can't," I said, tearing up.

"I promise you he is not going to live here with us. We plan to help him get a house out near the creek," she said smiling. She was trying to assure me she could control the situation. She continued, "You are a wonderful person. Just be courteous to Uncle Bill. He told me he made some mistakes because of his drinking, which was a result of your mother's illness. He was lost and didn't know how to react," she tried to explain.

"You can believe that if you want. I was there. I went night after night to get him out of the bars. He knew what he was doing. I can't live with him. I have done my best to forgive him; but I won't have him be a part of my life again; not this soon; it hurts too much right now," I said, trying to establish my boundary.

"We can help him try to regain your respect. Your father and I will put Uncle Bill in a motel tonight and help him get a house tomorrow. We want you to know how important you are, and we will not let him interfere with the family we have created," she said, again reassuring me of my place within my new family.

"I have to go to the library quickly before it closes," I said. I needed to get away for a few minutes to regain my composure.

"Don't be too long. Dinner will be ready in about forty minutes," she said, now moving away from my bedroom door. I picked up my binder and keys. I walked back through our house.

"I won't be long. I just need one book. I have it reserved," I said, walking out the front door. As I got to my car, Uncle Bill was standing next to it smoking. I did not speak as I approached him.

"This yer car? Guess Alma musta give it to ya. Looks like she is good to ya," he said.

"No one gave me this car. I am making payments on it and I had it before I moved here," I explained as I moved to open the driver's side door. He moved directly in front of me and the car.

"Look boy, you can't win if you start a war between you, me, and Alma. I was good to her and she loves me. She has loved me for longer than you are old. I got her right where I want her. She gonna make my life easy. You don't have to like me, but you better be nice to me around her or all this new wealth you done found will come to an end. Your old pappy knows how to get his way," he bragged, moving to the side of the car so I could get in.

"I have always been nice to you; some might say too nice. You do what you want to with Alma and Skip, but you leave me out of your plans. I want nothing to do with you. I will say hello, if people are around, but that is all you get. If no one is around, don't talk to me. Is that understood?" I asked, closing the door, and starting the engine.

"Come on. I may have to take this little car from you like I did at the hospital," he said, smiling and blowing smoke toward my window.

"I won't let you win this time. If you even think about hitting me again, you will find yourself on the losing end," I promised, backing out of the driveway. I knew he was evil and manipulative. I would not be forced to have him be a part of my life again.

When I returned from the library, Uncle Bill was sitting in the garden area with one of the ladies who worked at the rest home. We called her "Bananas" because she ate at least five bananas every day. She was a hard worker, did not smoke, had no family, and was not well educated. She was always cheerful. She went out of her way to help everyone.

I was surprised to see her with Uncle Bill. I was used to seeing drunken women, or at least heavy drinkers, with him. The next few weeks I saw them together more and more. Each time I saw them it looked like their friendship was headed in a more romantic or lustful direction. He would deliberately move closer to her when he saw me coming near them. She would usually try to play if off or ask him to stop.

* * * * *

We were having dinner one Sunday when mother made the following announcement: "Uncle Bill and Bananas have decided to move in together. It has happened fast, but both seem very happy. She can help us take care of Uncle Bill and he will have companionship," she declared.

"He seems to need constant companionship. I hope she knows what she is getting herself into with him," was all I had to say.

"They are both adults and capable of making their own decisions," mother said as she begun passing the various dishes she had prepared for dinner.

About two weeks later I found mother sitting in the dining room of the rest home crying.

"What's the matter?" I asked.

"You haven't heard about Bananas?" she asked.

"No, what?" I asked.

"She died last night in her sleep. Uncle Bill found her dead this morning when he woke up," she explained.

"Do we know the cause?" I asked.

"It looks like her heart just gave out. She had not shared with me that she had a heart condition. It looks like she didn't get the digitalis she needed," mother said tearfully.

Three weeks later mother shared the following news regarding Uncle Bill: "He met a lady named "Billie" at one of the bars in town and they went to Martinez and got married. So, we now have Uncle Bill and Aunt Billie," she said.

"We should wish her the best. She will need it," I said.

Mother and father had helped him get a house just outside of town, where he had lived with Bananas and now with Billie. I was instructed from time to time to take him places and to become a part of his life when he needed transportation. My new parents and I argued for almost the entire time since he had reappeared.

* * * * *

When I returned home from the Western States Tournament, Sandy, mother, and father were excited and proud of my accomplishments. I shared with them that I had only one last tournament the following weekend and would then have three weeks with no speech or theatre commitments. Without these excuses, it would be more and more difficult for me to avoid assisting with Uncle Bill. My problem came to a head the night before my last speech contest. Mother asked me to run some errands for her, purchasing certain items that I was sure she had never purchased before. I did as I was instructed because she said they were needed. I returned home with the items.

"Thanks for getting all of these things. I know it was time consuming. I asked you to make these purchases because Uncle Bill needs them, and I want you to take them to him. I told him you would be there soon with these items because he was important to us and to you," she said.

"You had me run all these errands and buy these things for him, knowing how I feel about him? I won't take them to him. I get sick to my stomach when I am around him. He is only manipulating you. He will take advantage of you someday. I have tried to be a dutiful son and earn your love and affection. I think it is too much for you to force me to deal with him when, as a young adult, I cannot do it. So, I am telling you that I refuse to go out there and to continue to associate with him.

You can do what you want with him. It hurts me too much," I said. I did not expect to hear what mother said next.

"You have to love Uncle Bill. He is your father and you will do as I ask," she said. She walked over to the front door and motioned for me to take the purchases to my car.

"I won't do it. I am sorry. I love you but cannot do what you are asking," I said, now emotional and starting to cry. Mother took a deep breath.

"If you can't do this then you can no longer be a part of this family. We must learn to get along with each other through the good and the bad. You decide what you want to do," she said as she placed her hands on her hips.

"I can't do this. I don't want to and not one person, not even you, can force me to associate with him and become a part of his life," I said, while my body was shaking uncontrollably, and I was feeling lightheaded.

"Then you need to leave," she said with tears in her eyes.

"I have my last speech contest tomorrow. It is just a one-day contest. I will have to get gasoline tomorrow morning and drive to Stockton. We are going to Turlock tomorrow for the contest. When I return, I will pack my car and leave if you have not changed your mind," I said, trying to give some time and distance before making any ultimate departure decision.

"You will no longer be a part of this family. It ends right now if you walk out that door. I will get on the phone immediately and cancel your ability to buy gasoline or anything else. We will keep your car here for when you come to your senses," Mother said.

"That car is in my name," I reminded her.

"The insurance is under our policy. One call and you will be driving without insurance and that is against the law. I will take you to San Joaquin Delta in the morning because I know it is important to you. When the contest is over and you return, I will drive back to the college and pick you up. Then when we get home, you, your father, Uncle Bill, and I can get together and work out how you are going to live with us, helping Uncle Bill become a part of this family," she stated, trying to reach some sort of compromise.

"I lost one car to him. I guess it is happening again. I will leave all my possessions here. When I get to wherever I move, I will send money for you to mail me my things. I won't be treated like this. I am trying to respect you; you know I love you; but you are making it very difficult for me. You are asking too much of me. You made me a member of a loving family, but now you are destroying it," I said, as I walked back to my bedroom. I changed into the suit I would need to wear tomorrow and walked out the front door. I did not know where father or Sandy were. I thought that if had they been there, they would have helped Mother see things as she should have.

I walked down Dainty Avenue toward Highway 4 for the twenty-mile trip to Stockton. With each step I took, I wanted to look back to see if my mother or father were pulling up beside me to ask me to return home. Just before I got to the first levee bridge, a car pulled over and the driver asked if I needed assistance.

"You aren't hitchhiking, and you are dressed in a suit, so you don't look like you are running from the law; so, do you need a ride?" asked the driver. I did not want to share too much, but I certainly appreciated the acknowledgement that I did not appear to be a criminal. I quickly assessed the car and the person talking. It was a newer car and the front seat was occupied by two people: the gentleman talking to me and a woman who was smiling.

"I have a speech contest in the morning in Stockton and I can't get my car to make this journey today, so I decided to get there on my own," I said.

"If you like, I can go back and see if I can get your car running; I am a pretty good mechanic," said the driver.

"That won't be necessary. My parents won't be available until tomorrow. Then I will call home and my mother will come and get me," I said, trying to combine truth and fiction as closely as possible.

"In that case, hop in the back and we will take you to Stockton. We are on our way to Sacramento, so it is right on our way," he said. I opened the back door to the car and sat down, fully appreciative of people being caring for each other. I had never picked up a hitchhiker myself and this show of kindness softened my heart immediately to their situation.

"My name is Herbert, and this is my wife Stephanie. Where in Stockton are you headed?" he inquired.

"We are meeting at San Joaquin Delta College on Pacific Avenue, next to UOP. I don't expect you take me all the way. You can let me off just as we get into town," I suggested.

"Nonsense! We have plenty of time and besides, if our son or daughter were stranded, we would hope a good Samaritan would come to their rescue, wouldn't we honey?" he asked.

"We sure would," she agreed. We talked all the way to the college. I thanked them again once we arrived.

I spent the night at a Motel 6 near the college. I competed the next day without sharing with anyone my immediate plight. I took second place in persuasion and first in oral interp. Once we arrived back to the campus from Turlock, I called home intending to clarify my family situation. My father answered the phone and told me he had been told by mother about the "misunderstanding." He also told me to wait for him to drive to the campus to pick me up. When he arrived, the first thing I noticed was that he was by himself. He smiled and motioned for me to get into the car.

"I don't know what happened, but I am sure we can work out this situation. You know we love you," he said, as I buckled my seatbelt. He would never drive until all passengers were buckled up.

"I cannot deal with Uncle Bill. He is only my biological father; you are my father now. I will do anything either you or mother ask me to, except for this one request," I said, trying to show a willingness to work around it.

"Can you take Sandy with you and from time to time take him things or make short visits? Alma is convinced that with time, things will be better, and he will be more responsible. Can you find it in your heart to do that much?" father asked.

"Sorry, I can't. At this point in my life I don't want any harm to come to him but being around him is harmful to me. I will go away until he leaves. That is the best I can do. I will come and visit if you want; I can write, even call. How does that sound? Can you support that position for me with mother?" I asked.

"You know how stubborn she can be when it comes to doing things with family. She has always forgiven her mother and brothers even when they do destructive things. I think she will demand that you leave. She feels that is the one thing you don't want, and it is therefore her ace in the hole. I will support your decision, but we will have to communicate secretly. She doesn't want you to contact any of us if you leave. You will have to visit Sandy while she is at school until this situation blows over. I will talk with Sandy and let her know how the two of you can communicate. I agree with you that Uncle Bill is a manipulator and in time his actions will tick her off and she will see that what she is demanding is unreasonable and will ask you to forgive her. I just hope you will find it in your heart to do so," Father spoke, helping plan a strategy of how to deal with her and her unreasonable demands. We did not talk about what was about to happen for the rest of the drive home.

When we arrived there, my mother was still insistent that Uncle Bill and I had to become family again. I called my sister Nellie and asked permission for me to return to Bakersfield to stay with her family until I could complete my Associate of Arts degree. She talked it over with her husband Leo and their two sons, Larry and Terry, and they agreed to let me stay with them. Father was insistent with mother that I be allowed to take my Mustang with me, and they would keep insurance on it for one month while I was transitioning from Antioch to Bakersfield. My exit from their home was difficult for all concerned. Both mother and I thought we had the high ground. My professional training after many years suggests there are times when one needs to stand their ground; but perhaps I could have done it differently and not have had to be so far apart from my family.

I called Coach Vogler and shared with her what was taking place in my personal life. She had been through a divorce recently and was very supportive of my decision not to subject myself to being around my biological father. I thanked her for all the training and teaching she had offered me. She insisted that I enroll in the community college in Bakersfield and continue my forensics activities there.

Many years later when I was president of the Statewide Community College Association, the union which also represented the faculty of San Joaquin Delta College, I was able to present an award to Ginger Vogler for being an inspirational and outstanding teacher and for her many years of service to students. That was one of the highlights of my professional career.

A more personal moment came a few years later when her family asked me to be the one to present her eulogy at her celebration of life ceremony. Ginger had left instructions that I was to be contacted to see if I would be willing to be the sole speaker at her service. She stated that the award I had given her had touched her so much that she wanted me to speak and then place her award in her coffin. All I had to do was share the love with others she gave to so many while she was alive. Many of per past students, faculty, administrators, and family members attended that great day. I will always cherish it as one of my happiest days because I was able to give back to her a small piece of gratitude for what she had taught me. By the way, her hair looked marvelous.

CHAPTER TEN

I promised Nellie and Leo I would only be staying with them about seven months while I completed my AA degree and then I would be transferring to a four-year college, leaving the Bakersfield area. My rent payment would be to style Nellie's hair whenever it needed fixing; and cutting and trimming Leo's, Terry's and Larry's hair as needed. Nellie went from having her hair look as though she did it herself (she did) to having a top ranked expensive stylist doing it. Cutting and doing hair for the family was quite easy and was something I would have done for free.

The semester had already started when I arrived. I was able to get accepted into the college three weeks into the term. Semester terms were fifteen weeks of classes and one week for finals. Bakersfield College's forensics program was known for debate and not as strong in individual events (IE). Our coach was Mary Copelin, a very caring but strict coach. Perhaps that is why she was such a good debate coach. There were seven people participating in the program. At my first meeting with the team, Dr. Copelin shared with us that the college only had the funds to send six people to the state and national finals competitions. She also warned us that at least two of those six people would be one debate team. If she decided to send two debate teams, then only two individual events people would be able to attend these tournaments. It was a small team that now with my addition suddenly was growing. She also informed us that any of us who were participating only in individual events would have to compete in two events and would have to place or go to the final rounds in at least two tournaments before being allowed to go to the state tournament.

None of the students doing only IE had been to a final round that year. I had already qualified, however, by winning my events while I was at Delta. I made it a point to go to every practice session she set each week for us to be coached. I also made myself available to listen to and help the other students whenever possible. I shared with her about going to beginning speech classes at Delta to deliver our speeches, an activity that could benefit both us and those students who were writing similar speeches for their classes. She loved the idea. Her team had never done that before. Of course, I gave Coach Vogler credit for suggesting it to me.

*   *   *   *   *

Not only was I working at a beauty supply company, I started an evening business selling women's clothes as a consultant with "Queens Fashion Clothing," which specialized in pant suit outfits, lounging attire, and informal dresses. It was a home party program, structured like Tupperware, where the host invites guests over for a showing and could win an outfit for hosting the event. I added an element that none of the other consultants had as part of their arsenal. I hired a model to show the outfits so I could talk about each one as it was being shown, and I also created a distinct hair style for each outfit by having my model wear wigs I would style ahead of time. By combining wigs, make-up, and accessories that could be purchased separately, this unique program began producing good results.

My model, Margie, was a legal secretary for one of the top attorneys in town. She had aspirations of becoming a congressional staff person. Not only was she pretty, smart, and charismatic, she had very long legs that helped immensely with modeling. She modeled for me because it was fun. She never wanted to pursue modeling as a career. She felt it was too cutthroat. She had been dating a staff person for one of the representatives in the state legislature. He had promised her he would get her an interview with a well-known and beloved state senator who could be her ticket out of Bakersfield. We became good friends, but I did not feel any romantic sparks going off. She was a woman who could have anyone she chose, so her sights were set, as she would often joke, on older, richer, and more influential men. I felt she was using her boyfriend as a steppingstone to gaining access to men with power and wealth. We would hang out after the showings with one of her friends, Nicki, who taught ballroom dancing and knew all the owners of the hip eateries and lounges in town. I was not yet twenty-one, but when we were with Nicki, I never worried about being carded. Nancy was twenty-two. One night we got really drunk at Nicki's house. The next day the two women joked with me about what we had supposedly done together. They would tell me things of which I had no memory; then they would start laughing and tell me they were just making it up.

Just before the state forensics finals, Margie came to me and informed me she was pregnant. She shared that this "bump in her road," as she called it, had to go away. It would derail her plans. She had been summoned to Sacramento to interview for a staffing job that would double her salary.

"I am sharing this with you because I need you to go with me to the clinic and I can't trust anyone else to know about my pregnancy," she said.

"I will help in any way I can; but you need to know I have great concerns about abortions," I said.

"It is my body and I don't want to have a baby at this time," she said.

"What about giving it up for adoption?" I asked.

"I would have to spend the next nine months here and everyone would know. I have already been told I have the job in Sacramento. I was told the trip there is just a formality. I cannot be pregnant and have a baby alone there. It will be all I can do to take care of myself. I am only asking you to drive me to the clinic," she said.

I had to think. By driving her, I felt I would be participating. "I don't know what to do. Someday I may very well be a minister," I declared.

"Are you going to decide which sins are acceptable and which ones are not at this stage of your life?" she asked.

"What do you mean?"

"Is it acceptable for you or anyone else who is eighteen or older to have sex as long as no pregnancy results?" she asked.

"I have not thought about it," I responded.

"If there is a sin, don't we simply ask God for forgiveness? I thought the only sin that could not be forgiven was to commit suicide because you aren't alive to ask forgiveness, right" Margie asked. "All I am asking you to do is to take me to the medical facility and when the procedure is over, I will call you and you come and take me home. Can't you do that for me?" she asked again sounding desperate. I knew she did not have anyone else with whom to share her secret.

I decided I would take her. Margie scheduled an appointment and I became her taxi to the clinic where she was going to terminate her pregnancy. When I went to pick her up after the procedure, she asked for another favor. She was short twenty dollars. She needed a loan and said she would pay me back by the end of the week. She left that weekend for Sacramento and never paid me back. For years I struggled with the idea that I had helped pay for an abortion.

*　*　*　*　*

Dr. Copelin wanted me to create an informative speech. Our team had five persuasive speeches but no informative speeches for competition. We met and after discussing various topics we decided for me to share with the audience something my sister Sandy and I had been trained to do. I wrote an informative speech on the duties and responsibilities of being an orderly and having to care for the dying patient.

I took the training and experience that I had learned the previous semester and created what I felt was a very good speech. It amazed me that in the terminal ward where we were assigned, you would have a day off, and then when you returned the person had passed and was no longer in the hospital. I tried to remember some personal examples of requests dying people made but did not get because it was against hospital policy or rules at the hospital. Two extreme examples came to mind quickly.

Many patients had been bedridden for so long that their entire bodies ached because they had been unable to move from side to side or up and down. They would ask for me to rub their legs or back. The hospital position was to deny this request because it might cause a stroke. These patients were in the last stages of their life, but I could not help them by simply rubbing their legs or back. Another example concerned smoking. Some of the patients had been smoking for their entire lives. Certainly, they could not smoke near their oxygen tank; yet, if their bed or wheelchair could be moved to an open area, why not try to accommodate them? No, it was against hospital policy. My speech won the next two contests.

After considering speech placement results, Dr. Copelin decided on the six people she would take to state and national finals. She decided to take two debate teams. That left two people for the other slots. With my addition to the roster, we had eight people on the squad. Math at any level meant two people would have to stay home. Dr. Copelin called a team meeting.

"I want you to know this was the most complicated and worrisome decision I have made in my entire life. I ran scenarios every way I could imagine, maximizing our best chances at both state and nationals. The two debate teams have improved so much and have been so dedicated I have to reward them for their efforts. That leaves four people and two spots. Again, I looked at results, attitude, growth, and potential placement. One of you did not qualify because of not placing high enough at the tournaments you attended. Now that left me with three people with two slots," she said and stopped long enough to take a deep breath. I raised my hand to be recognized before she continued.

"Yes, Ron," she said giving herself a bit longer before having to disclose her choices.

"As the newest member of the team and knowing through my interactions and our coaching and practice sessions how hard everyone has worked all year; and because I came late this semester, I volunteer to stay home and will be our team's biggest cheerleader," I said. The other students looked at me like I was crazy. The one student who had not qualified through the competitions began applauding my announcement. Dr. Copelin stood up and made a gesture for the clapping to stop.

"Please, let me finish. It was too difficult for me to exclude any of the last three. I went to the administration asking for additional funding. I got word yesterday, my request was rejected. I contacted as many of our faculty members as possible explaining our dilemma and why I thought it important for the college not to leave one qualified student behind. That would be like leaving your quarterback behind. Some very special people donated what they could. It was not quite enough. So, I am personally providing the difference. All three of you will be attending," she said smiling, and crying at the same time. We all jumped for joy. I never found out who would have been left behind. What was important is that none were forced to stay home. At state we won our first sweepstakes award. We were not so lucky at nationals and did not win any award as a team. I placed seventh in informative speaking. During the time from state to nationals, I had quit my jobs so I could concentrate on my speeches and I think it was worth it.

* * * * *

At the beginning of the summer, I knew I needed all the extra money I could earn. I got a job at Mr. Beefy Burgers, where my nephew Terry was working. We worked the evening shift together. Late at night, after the indoor dining area was closed to the public and only the drive-through was open, we would have fun, especially teasing younger customers. We created Okie voices and would stammer, stutter, and use unnecessary pauses to make taking the order longer. We also would repeat the order back, leaving out something so they would have to give us the entire order again. It was fun listening to them complain to each other in the car about how stupid they thought we were. We had one of the first drive-through windows in town and few customers knew that we could hear every word they said to each other. As we would give them their food, we would use our own voices and reveal something they had said about us while they were waiting.

One night I allowed Terry to borrow my Mustang. I had never allowed anyone to drive my car before; but we had become very close and I felt that if there were an accident, between him and his father, the car could be fixed. Unfortunately, he totaled my car when he hit an island divider and the car bounced into the oncoming lane of Chester Avenue and was hit by several cars. My car could not be repaired. My insurance did not cover Terry because he was not yet eighteen years old. My brother-in-law Leo gave me a 1962 Thunderbird. It had electrical issues and was soon replaced by a small Datsun two-seater with no air conditioning, although I was living in Kern County where the summer months registered over 105 degrees on a regular basis.

I also worked most weeknights at a liquor store, where I was told to card any woman, buying any type of alcohol, who looked younger than fifty. I was told it would make them happy and they would return to buy more. The store owner had a Studebaker Avanti, which she wanted to sell. It was a car ahead of its time in sleekness and style. It was a 1963 luxury model with wonderful air conditioning. Only 3,834 Avanti's were made that year. It had been her ex-husband's car, which she had received as part of her divorce settlement. When she found out I would be moving away, and she would not have to look at the car any longer; she sold it to me for only two hundred dollars. She allowed me to work one extra hour each shift at double time to work off what I owed. I did not have to pay any money out-of-pocket for the car. I found the original sales contract in the glove compartment. Her husband had paid $4,465 for the car in 1963. The Chevy Corvette Sting Ray was priced at $4,252 during that same year. I had to promise to take it with me and she did not give me the keys until the day I moved from Bakersfield. I gave my nephew the Datsun. The Avanti turned out to be a high maintenance automobile, needing an owner who had many more liquid assets than I did during my tenure as a student at Fresno State. When the transmission went out and I was told it would cost over a thousand dollars to replace it, I wound up selling it to one of my professors. I used those funds to buy a pre-owned Oldsmobile that allowed me and four other students to drive back and forth to tournaments in comfort while we were competing away from our own campus.

My nine months in Bakersfield were difficult to say the least. I had gotten a full-time job at a beauty supply house in January. My manager knew I was attending the local community college full-time since I had mentioned it as part of my application. The owner of the company, who oversaw a supply business in Fresno and this one in Bakersfield, had sent word to my store manager that I had to either quit college or give up my job. This was difficult to understand. The job entailed visiting with barber and cosmetology establishments and taking orders on the supplies they needed for their businesses. I had sold more supplies in my first week than any other salesperson at either location had done in a month's time.

* * * * *

On a Thursday afternoon my manager made an appointment to see me at 4:00 p.m. I arrived a few minutes early and she led me into her office.

"I am going to read you a letter I have received from the owner of our company. He never went to college and does not see the advantage or good it does. He started this business with only a high school education and has become a millionaire. He wants all the people who work for him to be full-time employees," she reported.

"I work harder than any full-time employee. I start two hours before the company opens. I make my calls during the slower part of the day or early morning, and early evening right before closing. I think my sales speak for themselves," I replied.

"I am on your side. It is his policy; not mine," she admitted.

"I won't quit going to college. I don't plan on selling beauty and barbershop products for the rest of my life. If you force me to make a choice, I am going to choose college. I will find another job. I like this one because it allows me to attend my classes and to call on my clients when I can fit them into my schedule," I told her.

"Let me finish. I must read you the letter. Let me do that right now. Just listen to it. We will talk once I have done as I have been instructed," she said trying to calm me down.

"It has come to my attention that one of our employees in the Bakersfield office is attending college while being employed by our company. That is not acceptable to me nor does it follow the guidelines I have established for the company. No one can work full-time and give us the time, energy, and dedication we deserve and go to college at the same time. Please contact this employee and inform him he must make a choice to be a salesperson or go to college. He cannot do both," the letter concluded.

"I know you can do both. I am going to report back to the boss that I read the letter to you and we had a discussion regarding your full-time commitment to the company. I am going to let him know his instructions were understood by both of us and he has nothing to worry about," she said.

"He has plenty to worry about. I am a great salesperson and he is willing to let me walk away. I must attend college," I protested.

"Notice how I worded my report to him. We have had this discussion. I have told you the company policy is to be full-time. I certainly think you are putting in a full week's work. None of the other salespersons are working any weekends, mornings before we open, or after we close. You going to college will be our secret," she said crossing her heart.

"I don't want to get you into trouble," I said.

"You won't. I have done what I as manager must do. I have read you the letter from the owner and told you our policy. If you can do the work; perhaps we can convince him later some people can do both. If going to college interferes with your productivity, then I will personally ask you to leave our company. Is that understood?" she asked.

"You will not be sorry for your decision. If for some reason, it becomes known I did not follow the terms of the letter, I will take full responsibility," I said in the most polite and apologetic tone I could muster.

Near the end of May, all employees were given a letter inviting (forcing) them to attend a recognition ceremony in Fresno. June 2, my birthday, was also the owner's birthday and he was giving rewards and special recognition certificates to employees who had made major contributions through sales. With the help of my sales, my manager was going to receive a thousand-dollar bonus for supervising our staff of ten salespersons, who had done better in sales volume than the Fresno store with twenty-five employees. I was told secretly that I was going to be receiving the top salesperson award. It was given to the employee who had the most sales volume from June to June. I had only been with the company five months. I was certain that my sales volume would change the owner's policy regarding the company and attending college.

June 2 arrived with our entire team going to Fresno for the celebration. It was quite an occasion. The owner's son was introduced as the new CEO of the company. His father gave a speech about how fortunate it was for him that his son had chosen to follow in his footsteps. We ate a better than average banquet dinner. Finally, they got to the rewards for top salesperson. The owner read from a script:

"We not only met but obliterated the goals we set for volume this year. Each one of you made this happen. I am pleased to announce that we surpassed every sales goal in every category. We sold more product than at any time in the history of this company. The top sales award was very close. Only one-hundred-fifty dollars separated the first place from the second-place winner. It is ironic that I had to send a letter to the recipient of our highest honor, during his first month of his affiliation with us, informing him that he had to choose to be a full-time employee with no other commitments or he had to leave the company. We are glad he chose to work full-time because within five months he is our top salesperson. Ron Reel, please come forward. You have won a five-hundred-dollar gift certificate and a plaque that reads, 'Top Salesperson for 1970' that will be hung on the wall of our main office."

I went forward and accepted the award because I had won it and deserved the recognition. After the ceremony ended, I approached the owner who was waiting to congratulate me again personally.

"I cannot tell you how proud I am of your contributions to the company," he said.

"I work hard and have many great clients who only needed to be shown why our products are superior to make their lives easier and their haircuts and perms better."

"I am sorry I had to give you that ultimatum, but we want people dedicated to one job and our company," he told me.

"About that policy, are you sure that it must be enforced? What if I were to tell you I did all of my sales during the time I carried sixteen units at college?" I asked.

"I would tell you just one thing. You cannot do both," he said in a manner not becoming of a CEO who had just praised his top salesperson.

"I have this certificate, plaque, and bonus check to prove otherwise," I responded.

"As of Monday, you will no longer be a member of our salesforce. Your last paycheck will be waiting for you. Check in with your manager and turn in your keys and any supplies you have to her. Is there anything else you have to say?" he asked.

"Only two things. First, I have shown through my hard work, your policy does not make sense and is not well founded. Second, Mrs. Smith read me your ultimatum and I decided not to obey it. She warned me of the consequence. She was right. This is your loss. I managed not only to go to college maintaining eighteen units, but I devoted more than forty hours to your job each week."

Deep down I believed he himself always wanted to go to college but was afraid to hire those who did because they might someday replace him.

"I can get another job. I am only working now to help pay for college," I said, as I walked away with the proof that some directives are meant to be ignored.

Rules should be made to assist people in doing a job in a manner that helps both the employer and the employee. One should obey any rule that is designed to protect, assist, and to make a job better. Mrs. Smith understood this, but her boss did not. I never did get to see my plaque on his office wall.

CHAPTER ELEVEN

I had been competing in the speech program at Bakersfield College for only one semester. I had gone to both the state and national finals. My speech, "Taking Care of the Dying Patient," had placed seventh at the national tournament. Counting the courses I had completed at Bethany, Delta, and Bakersfield, I had earned sixty-four units. I needed to transfer to a four-year college or university to complete my bachelor's degree. All the colleges I was considering had very competitive speech programs and offered both debate and individual events. Many of the students at nationals told me that they were going to be attending a four-week mini course in debate data collection, case development, and delivering debate materials in competition. It would be held at California State University, Fullerton, under the direction of Dr. Lucy Keele, who was recognized as one of the top debate coaches in California.

I had no debate experience before going to Fullerton. I knew it would be necessary for me to debate if I wanted the entire forensics experience and felt I would benefit from such a course. The class was a two hour and thirty-minute drive from Bakersfield. I had not driven in such a densely populated area before. I quickly made friends with the students attending the course, and soon the instructor and her assistants discovered I was one of the most dedicated students in doing research and in completing tasks they wanted done. When asked by Dr. Keele if I might want to continue my education at Fullerton, I told her that I did not feel I could move into an area that was as heavily populated as Los Angeles or the immediate surrounding area.

She suggested I might consider going to Fresno State and that I interview with the head coach, Dr. Hal Bochin. She was impressed with what was taking place with their program in both debate and individual events. She informed me that this new and younger coach had great credentials from high school and college speaking himself; but the most important piece of information she gave me was that his program appeared to be developing both men and women from a diverse population of students.

After the Fullerton class ended, I made an appointment with Dr. Bochin and drove to Fresno. The distance from Bakersfield to Fresno is about ninety miles. I wanted to get to the campus at least an hour early so I would have time to walk around the campus, talk with some students, and see if I could gain any insights into the forensics team.

After I pulled into a visitor parking lot, I asked the booth person where I would find the speech department. He gave me instructions on how to park closest to the speech arts building. I was impressed with how clean and well-maintained the grounds were. The grass was green and the trees tall and full. Most of the buildings on the campus were single story buildings. This provided a nice contrast from the Fullerton campus, where almost all the buildings were multi-level structures and even had a few buildings I would describe as skyscrapers.

As I walked to the back end of a Spanish style building, which was a combination theatre and speech building, I noticed two students sitting on the steps of the amphitheater behind the building. I wondered if they were drama or speech students. As I got close enough to hear them, I heard the girl say, "We should have a really good speech team this year. Bob and some of the other really good speakers are returning for individual events competition."

A young man sitting next to her chimed in, "We will be strong in IE, but also, this will be a very good year for us in debate as well." As I looked closer, I could see the two of them were filing what had to be debate evidence. I knew this only because of the course I had just completed with Dr. Keele.

"Hi! My name is Ron. I am thinking of coming to Fresno State this fall and I was hoping to meet some students who might share with me how they feel about the school, professors, and the speech program. I heard you talking about forensics competition, didn't I?" I asked.

"Yes. My name is Patti and this is Michael. We mostly do debate, but both of us can do some individual events," she stated. I reached out to shake hands with both.

"We are looking forward to having a productive year in debate, although the topic this year seems quite broad," she said.

"We have already spent a lot of time in the library, but it looks like we will be spending much more time there because of all the various kinds of topics people might develop into affirmative cases," agreed Mike.

"I know what you mean. I just finished a four-week course at Cal State, Fullerton, on understanding the topic, doing research, and how to present your side of a case in a debate. They gave all of us access to the materials that were developed by each of the students. I will bring all that information with me; and I plan to share it with my new teammates, if I decide to come here," I told them.

So, do you see yourself as a debater or as an individual events person?" asked Patti. She paused and waited for me to speak.

"I hope to be both. I want to excel in both areas. I have not had any real debate training, but I am eager to learn and think I have great potential," I responded, not very modestly.

"You made a great first step by going to a summer institute. We can certainly help you and will look forward to seeing what materials were collected at Fullerton," concluded Mike.

"I have an appointment with Dr. Bochin at noon. He does pronounce it "Bo Kin" right? Some of the people at Fullerton said "Boshin, Buchin, and Bosheen," I said, hoping I had pronounced it correctly. Patti started to laugh.

"He is quite protective of his name. He will respect you a lot if you pronounce it correctly the first time you meet him. Many people who do not know him mispronounce it until he corrects them. You will start off on the right foot if you know how to say his name," she said with a smile.

"What kind of a person is he? Is he demanding? Does he listen? Does he care about his students?" I asked.

Mike smiled and started to speak, but before he could say anything, Patti answered my questions: "He is very smart. I really admire his intelligence. He wants his students to demonstrate confidence in their presentations and, especially in debate, he wants them to know all the arguments on both sides of an issue. We all are assigned quotas for evidence gathering, but the amount depends on your level of experience.

He will really be impressed that you are bringing evidence with you. Of course, he will make us verify your evidence before we will be able to use it. He would not allow any evidence that is not legitimate to be used in a debate. In the classroom, he is quite demanding. Don't be late. He has been known to lock the door when class is supposed to start and if you are late, you won't get into class that day," she warned.

Mike started to laugh. "His bark is much worse than his bite. He wants to make you think he is demanding and all business, but outside of the classroom, we debaters have found him to be very friendly. He is often the butt of pranks, but I think he enjoys them," Mike revealed.

I looked at my watch, I did not have much time left before my first meeting with Dr. Bochin. I did not want to be late. I wondered if he might lock his office door if I were late, and I did not want to start out with that as my fate.

"It was great meeting both of you. I hope to see you again soon. If all goes well, I will become a member of your team and I hope to do my best to prove my ability and bring home trophies for us as a team," I said, as I started to move toward the back entrance of the building.

"Go through those doors and walk down and past the theatre classrooms, down the narrow hallway, and then turn left and go toward the end of that hallway. His office will be almost at the end. We have great coaches and we think we will have our best year ever. Hope you join us," said Patti.

I arrived at Dr. Bochin's office at exactly noon. It was quite a large office with two huge desks. I thought, perhaps, one was for debate and one was for individual events. I later learned that two professors shared this office. I was very naïve. The office had many trophies and plaques displayed around the room.

Dr. Bochin was seated at one of the desks. He was distinguished looking. His clothes looked like they were from a high-class eastern clothing store. He was color coordinated, and even his shoes accented his conservative appearance. He had a dark beard and mustache. I don't remember having had any teacher or college professor with so much facial hair. I had done some research on him before I arrived. I knew he had been a star high school and college debater. Austin J. Freeley, the well-respected author of the best-selling textbook on argumentation and debate, had been his coach and mentor.

I formally knocked on the door to his office even though it was not closed. He looked up from his desk and smiled when he saw me. He motioned for me to enter. As I moved through the door, he got up from behind his desk and moved forward and extended his hand to shake mine.

"Dr. Bochin, thank you for meeting with me," I said. He noticed immediately that I had pronounced his last name correctly. He smiled and waited for me to formally introduce myself.

"We are off to a good start. You pronounced my name correctly. You already have earned a gold star in my book," he said. Patti had been correct.

"I am Ron Reel. I just completed a class with Dr. Lucy Keele at Cal State, Fullerton. I hated the dense student population and the huge number of people living in that area. She said I might find the Fresno area closer to my liking and that you and your program were improving and moving upward in state and national recognition," I told him.

Dr. Bochin appeared to be appreciative. "It was very nice of her to say that to you. We are trying to make that statement a reality. Two years ago, we began a transformation here at Fresno. We have some extremely talented students returning this year and they will make us one of the most competitive teams in the state; but we definitely have room for another champion, if you find us to your liking and you feel we are compatible with you and meet your needs. We want to gather many students from various backgrounds to help in our pursuit of competitive greatness. Tell me about yourself, where you have been, and what you want to do if you transfer here," he said.

"Well, I am one of ten children. My parents were itinerant farm workers. I am the first in my family to go to college. My mother died at an early age and my father and I are not on speaking terms. I will be putting myself through college on my own," I said, feeling I had shared enough, but wanting to be careful to not share too much.

"Tell me something about yourself," I prodded. "Where were you educated and why did you choose to come to teach at Fresno State?" I asked. I had already done some research, but I wanted to hear the story from Dr. Bochin himself.

"I got my Ph.D. from Indiana University. Before that, I had debated in high school and college and acted as a forensics assistant at the University of Wisconsin, where I got my master's degree. I have done much writing about the rhetoric of historical speakers and tried to assess what made them successful. I chose Fresno because it is in California and doesn't have much rain and no snow. I also had a very small map and thought that Fresno was much closer to San Francisco than it turned out to be. We are a young faculty and our collective talents will provide a great education for our students. As far as forensics is concerned, I want our program to be known for both debate and individual events," he said. Dr. Bochin had given me answers that made me feel good, warm, and calm. Most of all, he made me feel that coming to Fresno would make me part of a winning forensics program.

"Well, I left early this morning and have to get back to Bakersfield sometime soon," I told him.

"Perhaps, we should get some lunch before you go. I was planning to go off campus. Would you like to go get some lunch with me?" Dr. Bochin asked. I knew I did not have much money with me. I really needed the cash I had brought for gasoline so I could get back to Bakersfield. I only had about five dollars over what I needed for gas. I did not know if Dr. Bochin was asking me to go with him to lunch or if he were asking to take me to lunch. If he were taking me to lunch, I did not have any problem as to where we would go. If he were having me go with him and was expecting me to pay for myself, I would have to pay close attention and spend a very limited amount of money in order to have money for gasoline to return to Bakersfield. I hoped he wanted to go to a fast food restaurant, but I thought I could always have something to drink and no food if we went to a regular restaurant. At Dr. Bochin's direction, we walked away from his office to the faculty parking lot. He continued to tell me about some of the top students who were returning to the forensics program.

"We have some outstanding individual events people. We have seniors who are outstanding in the exempt and impromptu categories. They were and are some of our best debaters. We also have some great interpretation specialists and platform speakers. One of our top interpretation people won many awards last year and is definitely one of the strongest competitors around. His name is Bob; I think the two of you will like each other and be good for each other. We have made a special effort to build up our informative speaking competitors. I expect we will qualify as many people to the national speech tournament this year as any other college. In what areas do you think you want to participate? I have tried to promote an atmosphere of sharing, learning, and helping each other become as good as they can be," he said.

"I want to concentrate on oral interpretation, persuasive speaking, and debate," I said.

"You are you telling me you want to be a triple threat?" he asked.

"I will do my best to help win as many awards as possible," I said.

"How are you going to finance your education?" Dr. Bochin asked.

"I will get a combination of student grants and loans. Perhaps I will be able to get some type of scholarship for forensics. A textbook scholarship would be great. I will also have to get a job. As I told you earlier, it is just me. I don't have any parents to help," I explained.

I can give you the name of the financial aid officer for the college when we get back from lunch," Dr. Bochin promised.

"That would be great. I have just enough time to go and try to get my finances in order," I said, as we were now sitting at a table waiting to order our lunch. I still did not know if I would be paying for my own lunch or if the good doctor would provide lunch for me. I looked down at the menu. The prices were much higher than Taco Bell, McDonald's, or Arby's. I was waiting for Dr. Bochin, who was a professor and who had heard my story about being on my own and not having any assistance from parents, to tell me he wanted to buy me lunch. I guess I should have told him more about my finances. I was too embarrassed. I did not say anything. He did not say anything about who was going to pay.

"I think I will just get something to drink. My nerves always kick in when I get excited or find myself in a new situation or before I speak. I am really out of my comfort zone with this visit and meeting someone as important as you. I have a difficult decision to make. Your answers and your explanation of the program are exactly what I think I need," I said. Dr. Bochin ordered from the menu. I just ordered an iced tea to drink. We continued talking. I explained how I wanted to learn to debate in addition to excelling in platform speaking and oral interpretation of literature.

He did not seem taken aback because of my limited knowledge about debate. I assured him I would take debating seriously and would be sharing the great amount of evidence on the topic that had been collected by the people at the Fullerton class. He asked me what goals I had for myself for the year. I remember saying I wanted to become the best. He told me he thought with me on the team we might win more sweepstake awards for the college than ever before. He also told me that he felt it was important for me to do well in my classes as well as in competition speech. We talked for about forty-five minutes. When the bill came, he quickly picked it up, looked it over carefully, smiled, and said, "You are certainly a cheap date. I hope you will join us."

I saw in Dr. Bochin, a mentor, a man who had it all together; and I felt I could learn much from him. We returned to the campus, continuing a conversation about the personal topics I wanted to discuss, and I told him about affirmative case topics that had been identified during my Fullerton class.

I went and met with the financial aid advisor. She shared with me during my visit she was going to be teaching a class in the fall called, "Black Psychology." She informed me she needed additional students to make the class go. I told her I would be happy to enroll. I had already decided that I would be attending Fresno State in the fall.

After meeting with the financial advisor and securing the funds I needed to use for my education at Fresno State, I went back to Bakersfield, knowing I was about to begin a journey that would change my life forever. I knew that Fresno State would be great for me, that Coach Bochin would become responsible for my finding the best in myself that was possible, and that some of the forensics students would become my best friends. It was a great day. Shortly after I returned home, I received a phone call from Dr. Bochin informing me that I had been awarded a small scholarship from the speech department that would pay for all my textbooks. Yes, it was a great day.

CHAPTER TWELVE

I moved to Fresno in late August and started my fall semester courses. I had enrolled in twenty-seven units, knowing I would drop at least two of the courses after the first or second week. I wanted to determine how each course would fit into my work and school schedules before making the decision to keep or drop them. I also wanted to evaluate the professor's teaching style, personality, ethics, and the expected workload for each class. More importantly, perhaps, I hoped to find a role model who would mentor me through the rest of my college experience.

My older brothers were more like distant uncles than role models. Dave was six years older, Joe eight years, and Leroy was fourteen years older than I. All of them had been married by the time I was eleven. They each had their own wives and families to support. I could not visit them very often and none lived close enough to be a role model for me.

When I first met Dr. Bochin, I thought he seemed to possess many attributes I had or wanted to have. I imagined I could have the material things he had if I would stay true to my career goals. He was educated, smart, independent, caring, giving, and task oriented. Other students had mentioned to me that no matter what city we were in for a tournament, he knew the location of the best restaurants and where to find the cheapest drinks. He loved competition whether in forensics, tennis, golf, or poker. He could be both rigorous and caring at the same time. He seemed like a viable possibility for my mentor.

During my first week at Fresno State, I decided to drop by his office to say "hello" and let him know what classes I would be taking that semester. There was a line to see him and it took a while before I could get him alone. When I was talking to him about how much I missed my family in Antioch, I happened to mention that the Nortons had provided me with, when I became nineteen, the first birthday party I had ever had. He was incredulous and said, "Are you telling me you never had a birthday party until you turned nineteen?"

"That is correct. My twin and I might have been given a present, and, perhaps, even had a cake baked for us; but we never were given a birthday party with others invited," I shared.

"I guess I was fortunate. My parents always made a big deal of my birthday and when I was in grammar school, they would bring cake and ice cream to school so the entire class could participate. When I got older, we would have a party at my house and ten or twelve kids from school would be invited," he said. "That type of display of affection showed me just how special I was. What can I do to make you feel special?" he asked.

"I don't need a party. I need someone I can turn to for advice when I have questions, a person who won't judge me for any mistakes I make. I need someone who will always share his honest thoughts and a person who will listen to my concerns, which may be different from those of most college students. I don't always feel I belong here. I have my doubts about my scholastic ability and how I fit into college life," I admitted.

"With the exception of your last semester at Bethany, you certainly fit into this college. Based on what you accomplished at Delta and at Bakersfield College, you are one of the most creative and eloquent speakers we have on our team. Your tournament winnings should quiet any second-guessing others might have about you. I have a lot of respect and admiration for all you have done, what you are accomplishing now, and what I know you will do in the future," Dr. Bochin proclaimed

"I think you probably feel obligated to say something like that," I told him.

"No, I don't have to say anything I don't believe or don't want to say. You need to start believing in yourself at the same level as I do," Dr. Bochin replied.

"I do believe I am great at styling hair, but this college has many more students who have more ability and are smarter than I am," I said, looking down and hoping Dr. Bochin would not force me to stand up for myself.

"You can play your 'poor Ron' game on yourself, but don't think it is going to work on me. I would not waste my time on you if I thought you were a loser or someone not capable of succeeding. I have a reputation for surrounding myself with winners. You will become one even if it is in spite of yourself," he said, lowering his voice for special effect.

"What if I can't live up to your expectations?" I asked.

"What expectations? You are limited only by the expectations you place on yourself. I know you can succeed. Would it help you if I told you I think you can win an individual event at nationals! But, let me share a secret. I can't control what happens to you. Only you can control your own destiny. Set your own limitations. Set your goals at the highest level. Only you can win or come close to winning. But unless you choose to try to be the best, you will never know if that possibility can become reality," Dr. Bochin observed.

"You want me to be the decider?" I asked.

"No! I want you to be a winner. I don't know if by winning nationals or placing second, third, or fourth will make a difference in your professional career. What I do know is that unless you decide to do the very best you can with the time and resources we will provide, you won't be happy. Get off your behind and let's start constructing your persuasive speech, then we can work on your delivery. Let's also be sure that you look like a winner. You must stop feeling sorry for yourself and begin to take responsibility for your own future. I am ready to see if what I think will happen does happen," he said, as he placed his arm on my shoulder. I knew from that moment on, I had a mentor for life. What I did not realize then was that a number of other students had the same idea. I was not the only one who wanted Dr. B's help. There was a reason I had to wait to talk with him. Getting his undivided attention would not be easy.

* * * * *

My next task was to find a well-paying part-time job. I did not want to begin cutting and styling hair until I knew my schedule and how much time I would have to work two or three days a week and whether it would be morning, afternoon, or evening. The only place I received a follow-up interview was with Tinkler Mission Chapel. It was a mortuary in the middle of town. The ad in the paper solicited a person to live on site, work the late evening or early morning shift, and to transport people from the hospital to the mortuary after they died; and then help transport them to graveside services.

My interview lasted fewer than ten minutes. Five of those minutes were spent filling out paperwork for employment. Three of the minutes were showing me where I would be living. Two minutes were spent listening to instructions of how to call the owner if there were problems that needed attention beyond what I knew how to do. I was introduced to the other night employee who was also a student, who was to allow me to shadow him for a few days until I felt comfortable enough to work the nightshift by myself.

Barry Harrison was his name. He was the first to start the conversation. "Hi! I am Barry. I am more than happy to share with you what I have learned during the nine months I have been working here. It seems there is a constant turnover with this job; most people only stay a month or so," he said.

"I am Ron. I don't know what to expect, but I didn't have any other job offer, so here I am," I responded.

"It is really an easy job once you get use to all of the freakiness. Let's begin by my telling you about the embalming room. When you are on the night shift and one of the hospitals calls to inform you there is a body that needs to be retrieved and brought back here, you take the black van; we call it the 'delivery van,' to the hospital. The staff at the hospital meets you, signs off on the exchange of the body (it is called the delivery exchange), and then they assist you to place the dead body into the delivery van and you bring it back here. Sounds simple enough?" he asked.

"Sounds simple enough if there was not a dead body attached to the assignment. What do you do with the body once you get back here?" I asked.

"If someone is here, like me or the mortician has arrived by the time you return, you get them to help you take the body from the delivery van and put it into the embalming room. If there is no other person here to help, you can either move it yourself or wait for someone. If you wait, you need to stay in the van so that you ensure no one steals the body," he said.

"Steals the body. What do you mean?" I asked.

"I have been told several bodies have been stolen in the past few years, so the new rules stipulate the driver of the van cannot leave the body alone. I always call the mortician as I leave and give him plenty of time to arrive before I get back, so I don't have to worry about staying alone with a body or being present if someone wants to steal a body for whatever reason. I won't put myself in the position of becoming a dead body myself so the thief would get two bodies instead of one," he said and then smiled.

"Is this story true, or are you just trying to scare me?" I questioned.

"I would never try to scare anyone at a mortuary. It is probably the safest place one can reside. Who do you know who would go to a mortuary unless they had to because of being notified of the loss of life of someone they knew? Let me tell you, one of the hardest things you will have to learn to face. Sometimes the bodies pass gas and move as *rigor mortis* starts to take place," he said.

"What do you mean, gas and *rigor mortis*?" I asked

"The dead body passes gas. It is not only foul smelling; it is also loud. Because the bodies are housed next door, and that wall is thin, you will hear it. If you go to check it out, you will smell it," he said with even a bigger grin, imitating someone smelling something putrid.

"I don't think I will be going into that room at night," I responded.

"I know our small apartment here is not much, but paying no rent makes the inconveniences worthwhile. The bedroom as you noticed has two queen sized beds; that means we will have to work things out if you or I have someone over when the other arrives home," Barry said.

"Sounds like dormitory living if you ask me," I replied.

"I am a psychology major with emphasis in abnormal psychology. You may find me with a female or a male. Don't be surprised. If you want to join us, please feel free to let me know," he said, smiling and laughing. By this time, I did not know how much to believe or how much of this conversation was for shock value.

"I don't think you have to worry about my joining you with anyone. Actually, I think we should work out a plan so that only on certain nights and with advance warning, either of us would be allowed to bring someone home," I suggested.

"If you have not tried a three way, you don't know what you have missed. But back to telling you about the job. We simply help the mortician with incidentals like equipment, supplies, shaving the men, and helping with the sprayer when needed," he continued.

"What exactly is the sprayer?" I asked.

"It is a hose used to wash down, or disinfect, or to take any debris that finds its way into the tub used for preparing the body for the family. The other thing you must do is to show the family and friends their loved ones when they come to view the deceased. You always refer to the deceased as Mr. or Mrs. whatever the name. The first time you meet the family will be in the viewing room. It is a special room that has special lighting, painted in soothing colors, is carpeted, has music playing, and has a water feature flowing so that one hears babbling water. It offers a tranquil setting, designed to comfort those who are seeing their loved one on what is probably the saddest day of their lives," Barry explained.

"Oh, one last thing for you to know. When you answer the phone at night, you need to say, 'Tinkler Mission Chapel, how may I direct your call?' in a voice that is not too soft, too loud, or too high. You need to make it sound professional and without much emotion. Would you like to try it?" he asked.

By this time, I did not know what to do. I just stood there trying to figure out what he wanted. "Try it! Say it out loud," he directed.

"Really? Tinkler Mission Chapel, how may I direct your call?" I said in an almost monotone voice.

"Perfect. Well, almost. You need to be just a bit louder. That is all the teaching I am going to offer you tonight. You are on your own. I am going out for a couple of hours," Barry said, as he gathered some personal belongings and left.

After he had gone, I began to wonder what I had gotten myself into with this job. The phone rang. I could not remember the name of the mortuary. I ran outside to look at the sign. Then I quickly ran back to answer the phone. Just as I was about to pick up the phone, it stopped ringing. I found a pen and piece of paper. I wrote down the name and what I was supposed to say. I sat in the guest quarters by myself. Even though I was twenty-one, I found myself afraid. I was scared of not doing the right thing if a hospital or a person called wanting information. I wished Barry had not run away so quickly. Baptism by fire was alive in Fresno. About an hour later, the phone rang again. I answered it. "Tinkler Mission Chapel, how may I direct your call?" There was a pause. I thought I may have said the wrong name. I looked down at my note. I had read it perfectly. Still no answer.

"This is Fresno Memorial Hospital calling. We need you to pick up a body. Can you identify this is the correct number by providing the four-digit code for your mortuary so we can proceed with this call?" asked the person on the phone. I was very confused. I did not know the code. Barry had not shared that part of my on-the-job-training with me.

"This is Tinkler Mission Chapel on Broadway. This is my first night on the job and I apologize, but the person training me had to leave for a few minutes. If you provide me with your phone number and name, I can call the manager and retrieve that code information for you and call you right back. Again, I am sorry for this inconvenience, but I don't know that information at this moment. I will get it and have it in the future," I said. The other person started to raise his voice.

"What do you mean you don't know the code? What kind of business is Tinkler running anyway? There are plenty other mortuaries we can call. You have just lost business for your owner because of your incompetence," the person said loudly.

"I am so sorry. There must have been a mistake. It is not the fault of this business. I take full responsibility for this mistake. I can rectify it, if you give me a chance," I pleaded. Then I heard someone else in the background who was laughing, ask for the phone.

"Ron, calm down. This is Barry. I was just initiating you into Mortuary 101. You passed with flying colors. I will be home soon," Barry said, continuing to laugh.

"I don't think that was very nice of you. First you leave, and now this stunt. We will talk about this more when you get back. Perhaps the manager should know just how much training you really gave me," I said and hung-up the phone. As I thought about what had happened, I calmed down and started to laugh. By the time Barry arrived back at the apartment, I was calm, but I acted really upset when he first arrived. I pretended that I was packed and ready to leave. In the end, we both made it through that first night.

A few weeks later we were called to one of the local hospitals to retrieve a body. We followed proper protocol and when we got the man into the embalming room, we noticed that his entire face was covered with facial hair. It did not look like he was growing a beard, it did not look like he was growing a mustache. It looked like he had not been shaved for some time. The rest of his body was quite hairy, and it looked like he had been on life support and did not make it. I was asked to shave him. I dutifully did it. He was a very good-looking man. I thought I had done a really nice job. We styled his hair, put him in the clothes the family had brought for him, and had placed him in the viewing room.

When his wife arrived, she asked for us to escort her to see her husband. I felt this would be a very difficult moment for her, but I felt she would be so happy to see what a nice job we had done. As was customary, I handed her a handkerchief, positioned myself to take her arm in mine, and proceeded to walk her down the aisle to the coffin so she could view her husband. I thought about telling her I was the one who had done such a great job of shaving and dressing her husband, but I did not.

"I just want to thank you and the rest of the staff. You have all been wonderful during this very sad time. You all have been so sweet and supportive," she said as we walked closer to the coffin. I deliberately moved my body so she could not see her husband for a bit longer. Then I moved to the side. We called it the "big reveal" moment. As I moved, she began to scream.

"What have you people done to my Johnny? What happened to his mustache? In over thirty years I have never seen him without it. My children cannot see their father this way. Quick, close the casket until this is taken care of. Do it now!" she demanded. I did not know how to respond. I did as she requested and escorted her to the manager. Thank goodness it was only about 3:00 p.m. and he was still on duty. After the manager calmed her down, gave her water, and asked her to meet the rest of the family that was on the way in the family room he walked briskly with me. As we left the room where she was meeting the rest of the family, he turned me around to face him handing me a one-hundred-dollar bill.

"Go to "Marty's Beauty Warehouse" down the street two blocks from here and buy a mustache to match his hair color, purchase some adhesive tape or glue and get back here and attach it to her husband as quickly as you can. I did as I was instructed and during that evening and especially during his celebration of life service, I prayed that no one would touch or kiss him because I was afraid his new mustache would come loose.

* * * * *

I had been working at Tinkler for three weeks. During this time, Dr. Bochin had assigned me a female debate partner. She was not a speech major; she majored in business. She was bright and articulate. Her parents owned one of the most successful wineries in the Fresno-Madera area. We were doing at least two practice debates a week. The graduate assistants called us, "Senior Novice" because we were learning so much so quickly. Unfortunately, she did not want to practice at Tinkler. Only once could I persuade her to practice at the mortuary. Even then you could tell from her voice that she was very uneasy. Mostly we practiced at school.

I was four days away from my first paycheck at Tinkler. My student grant and loan combination were two weeks away from being released. I had prudently tried to plan my funds to last until I got my first check. I had not eaten any food for two days. I could not even tell Barry about my situation. He had a big jar of peanut butter sitting in the kitchen and I thought about taking a few bites of it; but that would be stealing. I wanted to tell him about my plight, but he was always telling me how he could barely make it financially. I was not his responsibility.

From time to time my family had been on welfare. Momma would go and get cheese, milk, eggs, vegetables, and various kinds of meat. I looked up the address of the Fresno County Welfare Department and decided to drive down and ask for assistance. I parked my car beside several other cars directly in front of the office. I walked through the door and read the sign directing those seeking food stamps and assistance to the second floor. I took a deep breath and walked up the stairs. When I got to the top of the stairs, I saw a window with a sign that said simply, "Start Here." I approached the window. A large woman, who did not look like she had ever gone without ample food, looked up from her desk.

"Hello, my name is Ron and I need some assistance. This will be the third day I have not had anything to eat. I was wondering how I could get some immediate help. I only need enough to tide me over for two more days. Some cheese, a can of vegetables, and some meat would be great," I said. She smiled.

"This is the right place to begin," she said, as she took a pile of stapled papers from a stack on her desk. "Either take this home, complete the papers, mail them back or bring them back and we can start helping you," she told me.

"Is it possible for me to complete them right now and give them back to you today?" I asked.

"Well, if you want," she said, handing me a pen with the papers. I went, sat down, and completed filling out the paperwork. I only needed this one hand-out. I didn't see why all this paperwork was needed. I finished the paperwork and went back to the window. She looked up surprised I was back so quickly.

"Here you go. I only need a little to get me through until Friday when I get paid. I won't be back after that. Where do I go to get some food?" I asked. The welfare lady looked confused and got up from her chair and moved toward me to collect the papers.

"You don't get food on your first visit. It takes about ten days to process your paperwork and determine your eligibility. We will let you know," she said.

"But I won't need any assistance in ten days. I need help right now," I said.

"That is not how the system works, honey. I don't make the rules; I just enforce them," she declared as she walked back to her desk. I felt rejected, and embarrassed. Suddenly, I knew how my parents must have felt when they had to go and ask for assistance. I was so embarrassed that I had been forced to resort to asking for help and now I had been rejected.

I went without food until Friday. When I got paid, I finally ate. I also went to the grocery store and bought a can of potatoes, a can of peas, a can of peaches, a can of Spam, and a can opener.

At about 3:30 p.m. I drove back to the Fresno Welfare Department. I had my bag of items in hand. I approached the window and saw the same woman who had been unable to help me.

"Hello, remember me?' I asked. She looked up and remembered me.

"Your request has not been processed yet. It won't be ready until the end of next week," she said. I placed my bag of canned foods on the counter.

"I don't know if you have any idea how much courage, strength, and fortitude it took for me to come here and beg for assistance. I asked for just a small handout. You made it clear that you are just following your procedures when you did not give me anything. Now I have brought you a bag with some canned fruit, vegetables, meat, and a can opener so that should someone else find themselves in a similar situation to mine, you will have the ability on your own to help them. Explain to them about the waiting time, but then you can look like a heroine to them. You personally have a gift you can give them to help in the short term," I said, turning to leave that window and never to return. She called out, "We can't provide any service without authorization. We have rules," she hollered as I walked away.

"I heard you loud and clear tell me the rules for the welfare department. You, as a private citizen, however, have the right to be a person who cares about those who need help," I hollered back.

I don't know if she ever gave that bag of food to anyone. If someone found themselves in a situation similar to mine, I pray she did. Who knew it took so long to get help from your government?

I had been an employee of Tinkler Mission Chapel for almost a month to the day. I arrived back at our apartment about noon. I walked into it and sitting right on our dining room table was the smallest coffin I had ever seen; it held a baby's body. I did not know how to react.

I was shocked and angry. I called out: "Barry, Barry, what is this in our living quarters?" Barry was in the bedroom.

"We are full in all the bays, rooms, and facilities. I told them to put the baby's coffin here until we free up some space," he explained.

"What do you mean you decided it was acceptable for us to have a dead body, a baby, a dead baby's body placed in OUR living quarters without asking me first? This is not your sole domain. I would never have given permission. This is not acceptable. I cannot live in such a situation," I yelled.

"I don't see why you are making such a fuss. We are around dead bodies all the time. What difference does it make where they are located?" Barry asked.

"There's a fundamental difference between where one lives and where people who are dead are kept. I cannot live like this. I quit. I am going to pack my things and you, with all your stunts like this, will have to find a new pigeon to play with. You should be reported to the health department. I cannot imagine they would approve of this placement of a dead body," I said, as I made my way into the bedroom, packed my few belongings, and left. As I was leaving, I went to the manager's office and told him how I felt and why I was quitting. He did not understand what made me so upset either.

* * * * *

My immediate problem was that I did not have a place to stay. I decided to move into the forensics room at school for a couple of nights. When practice rounds were over, I would sneak back up to the room and crash. It was a temporary solution to the ongoing problem of where I would live during my college days at Fresno State.

Mike Weatherson, an articulate and intelligent student, was a year behind me in school. His debating ability was recognized by the other students as his way of becoming one of the top students in a very competitive event; but, more importantly for me, he enjoyed helping other students find what they needed to succeed in the very frightening and sometimes intimidating activity of intercollegiate debate.

The infamous day I learned from the Fresno Welfare Department that I would have to wait ten days while they processed my paperwork before being able to give me any assistance for food was the day before our relationship went from being student acquaintances to becoming friends.

Michael caught me staying in the forensics room early one morning after I had spent the night there. I shared with him that I had not eaten in a few days because of waiting to get paid. His openness and charity will never be forgotten.

"What do you mean you haven't eaten for a few days?" he asked.

"I don't get paid for a couple more days and I have run out of money," I told him.

"Why not call your family to get an advance?" he asked.

"I don't have anyone."

"You can't ask your parents?" he said, in a slightly louder voice than his previous question.

"My mother died three years ago. My father then abandoned those of us still living at home," I explained, in what I thought was a calming voice.

"I have never met anyone in your position. Are you making this up? Wait, are you telling me you have no money, no food, and no way to get food?" he asked in an even louder voice.

"It's not so bad. I will get paid soon. I just have to wait until Friday. I have nothing left at this time," I explained.

"Why don't you come home with me and have dinner with my family?" he asked in a caring manner.

"That is very nice of you, but I don't want to be a charity case. I can make it through until Friday," I said; but I was hoping he would insist that I eat at least one meal with him and his family.

"Don't be silly. My mom and dad are used to friends coming home with me to share a meal. I can help you with debate after dinner. My parents don't need to know about your being broke. We can even raid the pantry before you leave to find some peanut butter, jelly, and bread for you to take home with you," he insisted.

"Your family doesn't know anything about me. I appreciate your generous offer, but are you sure it will be acceptable to them for a stranger to show up for dinner? What if I don't fit in?" I asked, showing my lack of self-worth.

"Nonsense! My parents would insist if they knew about your predicament," Mike insisted.

"Do we have to tell them about my finances or lack thereof?" I asked.

"Of course not; they only need to know we are practicing for a debate and you just happen to be there at the same time dinner will be served.

My mother will insist that you stay and eat with us. She can be quite insistent. She cares about anyone our age who wants to be educated," he explained, describing a situation that always showed up when his mother thought young people were trying to better themselves.

"Tell me more about you and your family. Do you work?" I wondered.

"My father used to work for the "Laura Scudder" company, but when he was going into stores delivering "chips," he noticed that many of them did not have clean floors. He told one of the store managers how to make the dull floors shine and, as they say, the rest is history. He started a floor cleaning business and he now has contracts with a number of grocery stores. He cleans the floors at night after the stores close. I help him a few nights a week. That is my contribution, so they are willing to pay for my college costs. Mom keeps the books. My sister Joanie is dating and going to school in that order. I think she will be engaged soon. My younger sister, Katrina, is in the third grade," he said, helping me understand whom I would be meeting.

"You have a sister in the third grade? Was she adopted?" I asked.

"No, just unexpected. She is my greatest fan. I try to give her lots of attention. When I have friends come over to practice, she loves to listen. She is really smart, and her vocabulary is far greater than most kids her age. She has me as a model to emulate so, of course, she will be exceptional because of my contribution to her development," Mike bragged, not very modestly.

"Your family sounds very interesting," I told him after listening to Mike's description of them.

"Don't be late. My mother says people who are successful meet their obligations and timeframes. People, who are late don't excel because they don't respect other people who live by structure," he said, as he started to leave the room so he would not be late getting to his class with Dr. Bochin.

That evening revealed to me a family that still to this day is second to none when it comes to caring, supporting each other; and most importantly, offering true love to each person. As the evening developed, I felt I had finally met a real "Leave it to Beaver" family. I quickly fell in love with each of them. After dinner, Mike and I retreated to his bedroom to work on debate. Katrina sat on one of the two twin-sized beds in his room listening to us talk. From time to time, Mike would ask her if she understood what we were discussing. I was shocked at her vocabulary. Her explanations were as scholarly as those of some students in my college classes. She was so cute and smart. At one-point Mike used the word "pernicious" in a sentence.

"Katrina, what does that word mean?" he asked her.

The little robot-brained cutie replied with an answer that I certainly did not expect: "The use of 'pernicious' in that sentence is indicating that the harm described in the statement could be felt by the recipient," she explained. I was more than amazed by her grasp and understanding of the word. Not a single person in my family would have known the definition of 'pernicious.'"

Over the next few days, dinners and practice sessions became routine. I seemed to be having dinner and practice sessions at the Weatherson home on a regular basis. One evening Mike told me his parents wanted to have a family meeting with me present. I did not know what that meant, but I could not refuse because of their kindness to me.

We sat around the dining room table. Mrs. Weatherson opened the conversation, looking directly at me: "Ron, I hope you know we think very highly of you and what you are striving to do on your own. Mike has shared with us the situation you experienced almost two weeks ago and now we have learned that you have no place to stay. We met as a family and decided that we want to open our home to you," she said. I looked around the room. Joanie had a big smile on her face, as did Mr. Weatherson. Katrina not only smiled but was clapping her approval.

"I don't know what to say. This is the most gracious offer I have ever been given. You are all so caring. We will have to find a way for me to pay you something for my staying with you," I said. Of course, I accepted their offer. I lived with them for almost a year.

One evening at dinner, Mrs. Weatherson told us she wanted to share a note from Katrina's teacher. She read the following: "Mrs. Weatherson, I need you to help with a situation that has developed at school. Some of the other children are intimidated and frightened by Katrina's use of language. Her words like propensity, pernicious, causality, and cost-benefit analysis are words that most children (none to my knowledge) in the third grade know. If you can ask her to not use these words in school, her classmates will feel better. Thank you for your assistance in this matter."

Suddenly all eyes were on Katrina. Joanie spoke first, "I don't even know some of those words. Katrina do you really use those words?" she asked.

"We can't help it if Katrina is just too smart for her class," said Mike.

"OK, I'll try not to exhibit my vocabulary when I am with the less fortunate children in my class," said Katrina. Mr. Weatherson was now smiling.

"Katrina, you may use those words around Michael and Ron, but not at school. You will have to give your friends several more years before they can understand such concepts. You need to give the children a chance to learn at their own speed," he said.

Over the next year Michael and I became great friends. We shared many of the same aspirations and desires. Each of us helped the other become a better speaker. Our friendship became one of mutual respect and admiration. Eventually we both became college professors with award-winning debate teams.

That year taught me how members of a family may not always agree and may even desire different things but still support and love each other. Since that time, whenever I hear the "Leave it to Beaver" theme music or see Mrs. Cleaver on television reruns, I think of Mrs. Weatherson. She is a classy woman and a wonderful mother.

* * * * *

My relationship with my new mentor, however, was not progressing as well as I had expected. Without meaning to, Dr. Bochin had left me with a very bad taste in my mouth.

Early December found us traveling to the University of Southern California for the Pacific Southwest California Fall Championship Tournament. Happily, Fresno State captured a sweepstakes trophy and I managed in senior division to win persuasive speaking and I took second place in oral interpretation. In junior division we captured eight trophies. Dr. Bochin was so impressed and pleased by our performance, he announced that we were going to have dinner in Marina Del Rey and that if we would each return $10 of our food money, he would pay for everyone's meal. I had never eaten at a fancy restaurant before. I made sure that I sat directly across the table from him so that I could follow what he was doing and do the same myself. After we were all seated, Dr. Bochin rose and offered a toast to all of us.

"I want to let you know just how proud I am of this team. This is the first time in history we have ever won a sweepstakes trophy at the fall championships. We are surpassing where we were last year in the number of awards won in both debate and in individual events. You make my job fulfilling and worthwhile. Keep focused and we will make history this year," he promised. We all cheered and tried to tap the glass of everyone near us with our own glass. The server began taking our orders. I listened carefully to Dr. Bochin's order.

"I will have the prime rib, medium rare, the steamed vegetables, a baked potato with butter and sour cream, a cup of the clam chowder, and a dinner salad with bleu cheese dressing," he said. I thought the best thing for me to do would be to order exactly the same thing.

When the server came to me, I said, "I will have the prime rib, medium rare, the steamed vegetables, a baked potato with butter and sour cream, a cup of the clam chowder, and a dinner salad with bleu cheese dressing." The soups were delivered first. There were several different sized forks and spoons on either side of my plate. I watched Dr. Bochin and picked up the same sized spoon he did. When the salads arrived, I did the same with the forks. Finally, the main course was served. I looked down on my plate, and saw the prime rib and baked potato, but I did not know what the dark juice in a container was, nor did I understand why there were two containers of sour cream. I thought, perhaps, you put one on the baked potato and the other on the prime rib.

Again, I watched Dr. Bochin closely. I picked up the larger fork and saw him put some of his sour cream on his baked potato. He left the second sour cream untouched. I did the same. I was sure it did not matter which sour cream was put on the baked potato. Dr. Bochin took the large steak knife, placed it in his right hand, and used the bigger fork to keep the prime rib from moving, as he cut off a piece of it. He dipped it into the dark juice. I watched, thinking I had this formal dining thing mastered. I took my fork and positioned it into the prime rib and then took my steak knife, placed it in my right hand, and cut off a piece of meat. I dipped it into the dark juice. I put it into my mouth. It tasted really good.

I wanted to try the baked potato. I stirred the sour cream I had not used before into the baked potato. I took a big bite. I had never before felt my mouth get so hot. I could barely breathe. I felt my head would burst. Tears were forming in my eyes. I could not just spit it out because I was sitting at a table with about a dozen other people. I swallowed it as quickly as possible. I lifted my glass of water and took several sips, trying to wash down the hot taste still in my mouth.

I looked at Dr. Bochin. He had taken a bite of his baked potato. He was smiling and talking. Why wasn't he experiencing the same reaction I had? Perhaps, you have to learn to like the sour cream this restaurant served. Then I overheard one of the girls telling her neighbor to be careful with the creamed horseradish because a little goes a long way. I was trying my best not to show signs of being on fire. Then I heard Dr. Bochin say to the person next to him, "If you have not eaten horseradish before, be careful about how much you put on your meat. Just dab on a bit and then put the meat into the au jus," he warned. I wished he had shared that information earlier. I had placed the horseradish, all of it, on my baked potato. I could not eat any more of that vegetable. For the rest of the evening, I had an unpleasant sensation in my mouth and in my stomach.

Until much later in life, I did not tell anyone about what had happened to me. I now look back and realize it was quite funny. Years later I finally shared that story with Dr. Bochin. Instead of showing compassion for me, he laughed. At first, I acted like I was still mad about it, but finally we both laughed. It was truly a learning experience. When I became a coach and went with students to a nice restaurant, I always warned them about the horseradish before our food arrived. More importantly, I learned that before you blindly copy what your role model is doing, be sure you know why he is doing it.

CHAPTER THIRTEEN

Now, thanks to the Weathersons, I had food and housing under control, and I was ready to find the right salon where I could start cutting and styling hair. I asked Mrs. Weatherson to evaluate the top hair styling salons nearby and tell me where she had her own hair done. She informed me that the busiest salon around was called "Hair Fashions by Hazel." She reported that they had about a dozen styling chairs and that there was always a long wait to meet with a stylist, even if you had an appointment. This salon was known for providing haircuts and for doing long hair up for weddings and important school functions like proms. Mrs. Weatherson shared with me that she had learned from the woman who did her hair that the owner of Hazel's made specific demands about how many appointments her hair stylists had to complete each day. Mrs. Weatherson said that she went to a much smaller two-person salon where no quotas were imposed on the staff.

I drove by Hazel's several times, just watching the clientele going and coming from the salon. I wanted to see how they looked entering, but more importantly, I wanted to see how they looked leaving. It was a very busy salon. The building was situated on a corner, had a huge parking lot, and offered easy access from any direction. The only thing I noticed that would not work for me was the fact the salon was closed on Sundays. Sunday had always been my best day for having appointments. I phoned and asked to speak to the owner. I agreed to meet with her at 1:00 p.m. on the following Friday. I thought this would be a good time because it would probably be one of their busiest hours and I would get to see the salon in full swing.

When I walked into the salon, I found it was much different on the inside from how it appeared on the outside. It was old but had an elegance about it. It had once been a very affluent and stylish salon. There were twelve styling chairs that lined up along a wide aisle. One side had the styling chairs with a full-length mirror on that wall allowing the patrons and stylists to see what was happening during the styling. There were more than twenty hair drying chairs on the opposite wall. Towards the back was an open door. Behind the door a workroom housed six shampoo bowls used to rinse off colors, shampoo the clients, and offer an area for shoulder massaging.

A reception desk was to the left side of the entry. It had a semi-round granite topped surface with mahogany wood facing the front side. An elegant woman stood behind the counter. I guessed she was in her early sixties. Her hair was expertly styled; she had just the right amount of make-up, eye liner, and lip gloss for someone who knew how to accent her beauty. She was dressed professionally, telling any observer she probably earned a great deal more than the typical stylist behind the counter of a salon in Fresno.

"Hello, my name is Ron. I have an appointment with the owner. Are you Hazel?" I asked.

"I am Mrs. Hazel Hanson. None of my employees address me by my first name. I am called Mrs. Hanson by most, and the few who have special permission call me Mrs. H. I am excited that we are both considering your coming to work here. You have already decided it is a good opportunity for you or you would not have agreed to this appointment. I must now decide if you are a good fit for me and my girls. We have never had a male stylist before. I auditioned one about ten years ago, but most of my clientele at that time could not imagine a real man cutting their hair. It seems like it is becoming trendy to display one and you are good to look at. Allow me to give you a tour of our salon," she said.

"In all the years you have been open, you have never had a single male here?" I asked.

"I did not say I have not had a single male here. I said we have never had a male stylist here. There is a big difference. My late husband never allowed another man, who might excite me or my special clients, to hang around here," she said with a smile.

"Why change now? It looks like you are doing quite well."

"I think if I can find the right person, one who is energetic, confident, creative, and really outstanding, it just might be the right time to add another level of sophistication to my business. My personal clients are very demanding and many of them have lost their husbands and need a man, a young and talented man, who can style their hair and flirt with them; but who does not do more than tease them while bringing excitement back into their lives. The right person will help me keep clients coming here so I may continue to live the lifestyle to which I have become accustomed. Do you think you can keep my clients happy?" Mrs. Hanson asked.

"I certainly can," I responded.

"I should warn you," Mrs. Hanson continued, "I have certain other demands. I want you to take the styling chair right in the center of the room. Others can use it when you are not working, but when you are here it is yours and not shared with anyone else. You will charge a minimum of twenty-five dollars per haircut instead of the fifteen-dollar posted price. I will make a new sign specifically for you. If it is a short cut from very long hair, you will charge according to the amount of time it takes to complete. If it is a simple shampoo and styling, you can book six each hour."

"All this is fine with me. I have only one request for myself. My schedule must be Thursday evenings from 4:00 p.m. to 8:00 p.m., Saturdays, when I am not at a speech or debate tournament from 10:00 a.m. until 4:00 p.m., and Sundays from 11:00 a.m. until 4:00 p.m. When I must miss a Saturday because of a speech tournament, I will make up those appointments on the following Sunday," I said.

"I think that is acceptable," she agreed. "Now let's talk about salary. Starting out, the split will be 55% for me and 45% for you. If you become one of my top two producers within two months, we will change the percentage to 45% for me and 55% for you. After four months of outstanding production and if you're meeting the needs of my ladies, we will change it to 60% for you and 40% for me. I think I am being quite fair with you since I have never seen you perform. My stylists, who usually audition for me before discussing commissions, earn only a 50/50 percentage for their first year. I must be able to make enough money to keep the doors open and to provide the top supplies, so our clients stay with us and don't try another salon. Of course, most of your money will be coming from tips. I hear that most male stylists make double their salaries in tips. If you please my clients as I want you to do, you will find them more than generous."

"We both know you called my last employer and my guess is that she told you I am worth whatever I ask for. Right?" I asked.

"I did call. She told me you were self-confident, and she suggested you might ask for the world in our first negotiation; she may have mentioned you might be worth it. You must meet the quotas I provide for you and make our customers happy. If you don't live up to my expectations, I will send you back through the same door you just entered. If you can live with my rules, then we have a deal. And one last thing, when you go to those tournaments and win awards, I want you to bring back the trophies and display them in the salon for at least a week, so that our patrons can see why you were gone. Some of my ladies will want to see how their coming in on Sundays is helping you further your education. It will be great publicity for you and for the salon," she predicted.

"How many walk-ins or phone calls do you get every day?" I asked, trying to figure out if it was going to be worth my effort to work at this salon.

"We get more than enough to keep you busy. I will personally direct new and some of my old and cherished clients in your direction. Many of them have plenty of money and a new experience with a man styling their hair will make them quite content and we both will benefit in this endeavor. Your old boss said you specialize in shoulder massage after each shampoo. Is that still part of your *modus operandi*?" she asked, smiling, and giving me a wink.

"I know how to do my job. I will offer my entire bag of tricks to each of our clients and offer such a professional styling experience that they will want to return time after time," I promised

"Then I think we are ready to make an announcement and do some publicity about your arrival. Some of my girls may be jealous at first, especially my floor manager who watches over the other girls and makes sure supplies and money are accounted for. She will try to manage you, but you report only to me. Let her think she is your boss. After you raise the bar for prices of cuts and styling, the other girls will be able to increase their charges as well. All of us will benefit from my allowing a man to work here. You will make a lot of money if you play your cards right, but if you screw up you won't have a job here or at any respectable salon in town. I still have a lot of pull with most of the other fashionable shops. Don't get on my blacklist. The more all of you charge, the bigger the profit for little old me," she concluded.

It was clear that Mrs. Hanson was not going to let me have my way without earning it. She understood her position. We shook hands and I departed, knowing I would soon be making enough money to finance my education and to allow me to dress the part of a successful forensics competitor. What I did not realize at the time was what I would have to do to keep my job and to earn enough money for basic expenses and not have to depend on others for assistance.

CHAPTER FOURTEEN

On the second day of classes I arrived at my human sexuality class about ten minutes early. I noticed that one of the students, who had been in my communication course the day before, was going to be in this class as well. Her name was Iris and she waved when she saw me approaching.

I joined her. "Good morning," I said. "Are you going to be in this course also? Perhaps we could become study partners?" I asked, smiling, and hoping she would agree to my suggestion.

"Having a study partner is a good idea. I took this instructor, Dr. Roshay, last semester and he gave only three "A's" to a class of thirty students. I hear that all his classes follow the same procedure. He has you do a lot of group activities and projects during class, but your final grade is based on the four term papers he has you write. The activities and projects don't count toward the final grade; he says they are activities that prepare you to change your behaviors," she explained.

"I guess there can only be one other student who will get an "A" this semester. We will claim the first two," I said. By this time most of the students had gathered around the entry door to the classroom. The students were on time; the professor was late.

"Dr. Roshay expects you to spend a lot of time completing the papers he assigns. He seems to have a thing about associating good writing with the amount of time one spends doing research and writing the paper," Iris said. She continued, "I probably spent over forty hours just gathering materials for each of my papers for his class last semester. I always mentioned to him the amount of time I was spending on it when I would schedule progress reports and seek his assistance during his office hours. Are you that committed?" she asked, now smiling.

I thought for a moment. I wanted to fit in with the other students. If I told Iris I could read over 1,000 words per minute, she might think I was bragging and trying to suggest I was better than she. In an attempt to sound like a typical student, I responded, "Such an expectation is asking a lot. It is alarming to me for him to equate time and results. I can assure you I don't spend that amount of time when I do research. I must work at a full-time job as well as go to school. I spend about 90% less time doing research than most other students do," I said, again smiling, while trying to portray myself as an average student and to hide my superiority to most. With my reading speed, I could do my research considerably faster than other students.

Suddenly, she and the rest of those standing directly in front of the door moved. A tall dark-haired older man (around forty) wearing a three-piece suit was unlocking the door. He held the door open motioning for all the students to enter.

At least at the start of the semester, Dr. Roshay was one of my favorite teachers. His teaching style included a combination of lecture, group discussion, and one aspect, which I had never experienced before, which he called "group union or individual will." From the first day when he explained how the class was to be conducted and shared his syllabus, he went out of his way to let us know we would find ourselves in unique and challenging situations during the class activity section of the class. He wanted us to understand that experiencing something new could be exciting and rewarding. He also wanted us to feel that it was acceptable to stop participating in any activity that made us feel unsafe or very uncomfortable.

"This class is explicit," he warned. "We will talk about various types of intercourse between men and women, women and women, and men and men. We will cover the advantages and disadvantages of lubrication and discuss types of sexual harassment. We will also look at pedophilia, examine various views of abortion, and finally, we will consider gender identity. Some of you will learn about heartbreak for the first time, how betrayal may come about, and how one becomes jealous when it comes to finding out that a partner is not being faithful. These topics may scare some of you; but if you allow me to ease you through the emotions that will arise during this course, I will provide a safe environment to discuss, experiment, and gain respect for sex. In this class, you will learn how to express your wants and desires without harming physically or psychologically either yourself or a partner," he said, trying his best to calm as many apprehensions and mixed feelings as possible. Most of the class was younger than twenty-four; many of the students shared that they were virgins.

Some of the in-class activities consisted of us holding hands and asking questions of a partner about what things made them feel sexy or we found ourselves sharing what we might like to do to gain satisfaction. During this time, we could do no more than hold hands or share eye contact. I heard about many things I had not even read about. Some people talked about how they had done or imagined performing a certain sexual maneuver, and some even shared what they had done during their own sexual encounters. One of my partners revealed that she liked having her ears kissed and licked. One partner suggested that a very light pulling and twisting of a nipple was exciting. One day we were teamed up with same sex partners. There was nothing I could share because I had not had sex with a man. My partner revealed that he was bisexual and told me he experienced indescribable feelings and emotions when he was with another male.

During the remainder of the semester I began to think that Dr. Roshay was quite manipulative. We all revealed things about our past, present, desires, ambitions, marital status, some shared sexual proclivities, and finally we sought acceptance. Dr. Roshay did not share anything about himself, his family, nor his job outside of this class. It appeared to me he was a facilitator of the course objectives, but he was not participating or investing in the class to the degree he expected from his students. He wanted us to share our secrets; while at the same time he was not willing to share any of his own.

His four papers almost derailed my academic career. When we got our first assignment back from Dr. Roshay, I was shocked. My paper was given a score of "79" points and a letter grade of "C+" instead of the higher grade I was expecting. I thought Dr. Roshay might have made some type of clerical error. I wondered what the difference in his mind was between a grade of "79" and a grade of "80." One grade was a "C" and one point higher was a grade of "B." That one point could have a strong psychological effect on the confidence of the writer. To me it seemed more meaningful for a student to feel better about a grade of "B" than to experience the grade of "C." Iris got one of the two "A" grades given for the assignment. She had earned a point score of "95."

I was very concerned. I went to see Dr. Roshay during his office hour because Iris and I had read each other's papers and neither of us found any grammar, spelling, or content problems. We also made suggestions about the content found within both papers. We thought we made both of our papers stronger by sharing and critiquing each other. We had anticipated that similar grades would be given to our papers. Neither of us anticipated a lower grade for my paper.

"Can you share with me what you found so weak about my paper that resulted in only a grade of a "C?" How can I make sure that my next three papers are done so that they are scored much higher and are completed to the level that meets your expectations for outstanding work?" I asked him. He took my paper from my hands.

"You are no longer at a community college. You need to make sure you spend more time researching and reporting your work now that you are here; research and presentation of ideas are key components of outstanding writers," he said, dismissing my main concerns and not addressing the issues I wanted addressed as he returned my paper to me.

"Do you have any idea how much time I spent on this paper? I don't know how less time itself should result in automatically lowering a grade. Although I transferred from a community college, I originally started my academic career at a well-known and respected four-year college; my mother became ill and I transferred to a local junior college close to our home so I could help the family take care of her," I said.

"Evidently you did not spend enough time or research to satisfy me. Perhaps you should at least double your efforts for your next paper. That might give you more time to find better examples and to further your analysis," he said, now sitting at his desk but not establishing eye contact with me. "I think I have answered your questions; spend more time researching various points of view and present more in-depth analysis," Dr. Roshay replied.

I left slightly more confused than when I arrived. I could not figure how the amount of time I spent should have been a concern or justification for a lowered score. I also knew that he did not know how much time I spent because he had not asked me that question directly. I felt I had covered what needed to be discussed in the paper.

I met up with Iris in the library and told her what he had said. Neither of us could figure out what the time suggestion was supposed to mean. We both agreed I should increase the number of bibliographic entries because that would demonstrate increased time spent on the topic and provide a broader array of materials that he would see that I was trying to do what he suggested to improve my grade.

The second paper was assigned, and I made sure mine was submitted on time. I paid special attention to making sure it was organized and double spaced. I checked spelling, punctuation, and included a massive bibliography so he would see how many sources I had read for the assignment. It would have taken the average reader at least forty to fifty hours or more to read the articles outlined in the bibliography before the hours needed for writing the paper. I had done this to demonstrate the additional research that had been done in the preparation of the paper just as he suggested.

Iris received a grade of "96" for this assignment. My grade was a "89" for this paper. Again, I did not know why he gave my paper the highest "B" grade he could and not the lowest "A" that he could have given me. Fifty percent of the class was over, and I had earned only "84%" of the possible points. I knew I would have to earn much higher scores for the next two papers if I were to earn the grade I wanted and felt I should receive for the course.

I visited Dr. Roshay in his office, and he said I was improving but that he wanted to see even more improvement. He shared that he realized through my extensive bibliography I was spending more time developing my thesis and beefing up my examples because of the additional information I was uncovering. He suggested I look at the last two papers Iris had submitted to see the quality of work an outstanding paper included. Unbeknown to him, I had already been a part of her paper development. I had seen it firsthand. We had been working together on all our papers.

Nevertheless, I did as he requested. I reexamined our two papers. We had been research partners as well as editors for each other. I read hers and did not think either paper was any better than mine. When we got the results of the third paper, I was again shocked. My grade was "91" and Iris had earned a grade of "99." I had a collective grade of "86.33" for the course and Iris had a grade of "95.5."

Now I would have to earn a grade of "99" on my final paper to earn a course grade of "89.5" which when rounded would constitute the lowest "A" he would give. My grade was moving up with each paper, but it did not look like it was possible for me to earn the grade I felt I deserved.

Iris and I had been reading and helping each other edit our papers since before the first bad grades had been posted. I told her: "I think

Dr. Roshay has stereotyped me as a "B" student and is not going to give me my deserved score for the last paper or for the grade I should have for the course. I don't know how to overcome his prejudice. Perhaps it is unintentional, or it may be something the professor feels about my ability. I have tried to get him to share with me reasons for the continued lower scores, but I just get generic statements that have no real meaning. I really believe my papers are as good as yours," I said, as we were writing our rough drafts for the last assignment.

"There does seem to be something he does not like about your writing that prevents him from giving you the score I would give you and feel you deserve. What might we do to help you earn that "99" score you need?" she asked.

"I have an idea. You turn my paper in as your own and I will turn your paper into him with my name on it. You have earned a "95.5%" score thus far. He is now giving me grades that will not lower your total score enough to put your grade of "A" in jeopardy. This will be the true test as to whether or not Dr. Roshay is biased against me," I shared.

"I don't know. What if he finds out and charges us with some type of fraud? I can't afford to have my grade lowered. Some might think we were cheating," she said.

"This is not cheating. We are both writing our own papers. We will just put different names on the papers to see if name recognition is the reason for any type of lower score," I begged.

"I'm not convinced," Iris said in a whisper.

"This is the only way to know for sure," I insisted. "If it turns out as I think it will, he will have to see that he has subconsciously at best, and deliberately at worst, decided to prevent me from earning a grade of "A" for his course," I told her.

"OK, but we must not tell anyone else what we are doing until we know the outcome," she said. We turned our last assigned paper into Dr. Roshay. The paper Iris had written with my name attached to the paper was given a score of "96." Dr. Roshay had written that I was finally writing at the level he always knew I could if I put in the proper time and effort. The paper I wrote which had Iris' name was given a grade of "100." He commented on what he thought was her paper that it was one of the best papers he had ever had the privilege of reading. My score of "96" looked like he had recognized it to be one of the best in the class. Yet, it was that score that caused my total grade for the course to be 355 points for the semester which was 88.75% and rounded up was only a grade of 89%, which was a "B+" for the class. Had I earned 99 or 100 points, like the score given to the paper he thought was written by Iris, my score for the class would have been 358 or 359 points. Either score would have been enough to have earned either 89.50 or 89.75% when rounded would have been 90% and a grade of "A" for the course. I had earned a score of 100, but he thought my paper had been written by Iris.

I asked Iris to go with me to see Dr. Roshay. As we approached him, he seemed happy to see Iris with me. I started the conversation.

"I have tried very hard this semester to find out exactly how to write a paper that pleases you," I said.

Before I could continue, he responded: "You have made great strides. I can tell you are spending much more time on your papers and when you decide to research even more types of journals, and develop a wider scope of theories and positions, and spend just a bit more time developing and extending your examples and crystalizing your main points; you will earn all "A's" like Iris did."

"About that issue. I have never figured out what the amount of time I spend has to do with paper writing as long as one spends the amount of time he or she needs," I said.

"When one spends 90% less time than the others, he is not usually going to be at the top of his game or at the top in my class," Dr. Roshay responded.

"Why do you say that?" I asked.

"On the very first day of class, I overheard you say you spend much less time doing research than the other students do. I am one who feels time spent on papers is very important because it allows one time to examine a vast variety of views, allows different theories to emerge, and allows the writer time to decide the exact direction her or she wants to develop the theme," he said now rising.

I finally figured out what had happened. He had overheard the statement I had made to Iris trying to pretend I was only an average student.

"Dr. Roshay, the part you didn't hear, or I didn't say that day is that I don't need as much time researching as most students because I read over 1,000 words per minute when the average person reads between 200-250 words. I read five times faster than most other students. It appears to me that you decided I was to be a "B" student at best based on that statement. Such stereotyping is really not professional," I said, holding my breath to see how he would react.

"I don't think I did any such thing. I have always tried to be fair and open minded. I feel my instructions to you in the beginning of our class was beneficial because I saw you following them, and your writing improved. Your adherence to my requests has made you a better writer. You almost earned an "A." Had you earned a "99 or higher" on that last paper you would have just made a grade of "A" for the class," he said confidentially.

It was amazing to me that he knew exactly how many points I needed, and the grade he assigned what he thought was my paper prohibited me from obtaining the score needed to earn the grade I deserved.

"Well, I think I did earn enough points," I said.

"No, it was a grade of "96" he said. Again, it was amazing that he knew the actual points I needed and the amount that would keep me from the grade.

"Actually, the paper I wrote, which I turned in under Iris' name, earned a score of "100" from you. The paper she wrote submitted under my name was the paper you gave the "96" grade which was just low enough to keep me from the grade I deserve in your class," I said, confronting Dr. Roshay.

"Are you telling me the two of you plagiarized your papers?" he asked in a very loud voice.

"No. I wrote my own paper and so did Iris. Neither of us plagiarized anything in the papers. We were testing your ethics and your prejudice against me and you failed," I said just as loud as he had spoken.

"I think we need to go see my department chair; and when I let him know the two of you cheated by turning work into me that was not your own, there will probably be a price to pay. I think you both should probably earn a grade of "F" for this assignment," he said rising from his desk.

"If you insist, we will go with you to see the chairperson. I think he will also want to hear our side of the story. Our intent, my intent, is not to get anyone in any type of trouble. You are a tenured professor liked by many students. You are a dedicated and likeable person. Do you think it is possible you decided early in the semester I was just an average or slightly above average student? Perhaps it is something I said that first day when I was trying to portray myself as average to Iris. All I needed by the end of the semester was one additional point from the first three papers and I would have earned a letter grade of "A" from you without us having to come to you with what we did. Is it possible for you to reconsider my first three papers to see if perhaps you judged any one of them too harshly and that one or collectively, they might earn one additional point? The papers you just returned to us has me earning two additional points. That in and of itself should be enough to demonstrate what I can and should earn in this class. I just want my grade to be reflective of my writing and ability. I am sorry for falsely portraying myself that first class meeting," I said as he sat back down behind his desk. His demeanor seemed to change in that instant.

"I suppose I might have been predisposed against you because of hearing your statement about not needing to do as much work as about 90% of other students. It could have made me examine your papers more critically than the others. I try to judge each paper on its own merits; but I may have overcompensated in the wrong direction when it comes down to what I actually did," he confessed.

"I was wrong for suggesting to Iris and anyone who overheard my statement and construed that day that I don't take my education seriously. I wanted to fit in as a typical student. I wanted the other students to accept me and I was afraid if I told them about my reading skills, I would not fit in with most. I promise I will never do that again," I shared.

"I guess we both have learned something from this situation. I am willing to give you one additional point," he said smiling at both of us.

That one point resulted in me learning a very important lesson and saved my grade. Do not pretend to be someone or something that is less than you can be or are at any given time in your life. It also taught me to stand up for myself when I feel an injustice or mistake is or has taken place. I also learned that every point one earns in academic classes matters.

I never took another class from Dr. Roshay. I did not want to risk my grade again. I felt we both had learned from this incident and I hoped he would do his best not to be prejudiced against anyone from that point forward. I began taking my psychology classes from Dr. Holder, who later served on my committee for my master's degree.

CHAPTER FIFTEEN

I will never forget my first day at "Hair Fashions by Hazel." When I arrived, I learned that Mrs. Hanson had booked me for ten appointments, seven haircuts and three shampoo and styles. My station was ready and a laminated sign with my name was posted on the mirror that overlooked my station. The drawers to the styling booth were opened wide so I could easily arrange my cutting, styling, and weaving equipment, as well as the towels and rollers I would use. I would not have to wander around the salon looking for something I needed.

I had just placed my hair styling items into the places where I could easily access them, when I noticed a very attractive Latina woman, who was using the first styling chair when you entered the salon, approaching me. She smiled, extended her arm to give me a professional handshake, and looked directly into my eyes, "Hello, my name is Maria Vegas Batistas. You may call me Mary when we are here in public; but outside you will need to call me Maria. I am the on-site manager, overseeing the stylists. If you need assistance or if there is a problem, let me know and I will help get it resolved," she explained.

"My name is Ron. It is very nice to meet you. I didn't know there was an on-site manager overseeing the other stylists. Mrs. Hanson did not mention that anyone will be overseeing me. I am certainly willing to help with others in any way I can. But I will not need you to oversee me or my work," I told her.

"Let me reword what I said to you. I oversee the group of stylists' bookings, make sure walk-in appointments get quick service from a stylist, sign-off on final payment receipts before they are given to the client, and most importantly, make sure the register comes up with the correct amount of money that has been charged for services at the end of each shift," she explained.

"I will turn in my tickets to the receptionist to sign-off on the amounts, but I don't need anyone to oversee my charges or my work," I reiterated.

"I will be watching you today. Perhaps we can learn something from each other," Maria said.

"You may watch me anytime you wish; but please do not interfere nor critique my work in front of any of my clients. You seem nice and I certainly don't want to cause a scene here at work, but I only have one boss when I am working and that is me. If Mrs. Hanson is unhappy, she can have a discussion with me and we can decide if I will continue working here, but no one is going to suggest that I am not doing something correctly," I responded.

"Again, I will watch today and by the end of your shift, if I feel there is a need to discuss an issue with you, we can discuss it then," she stressed. "Part of my duty as the manager is to let you know you can turn to me if you feel there are issues, client problems, or product that does not meet or exceed your expectations," she said. You might want to remember that when walk-ins or new clients come in, they often ask me for my opinion of the staff and I freely give it to them. As she finished, she reached over and touched the side of my face and winked at me.

"Are you attacking me or flirting with me?" I asked.

"I would never attack a man. Usually I must tell them to leave me alone," she boasted.

"Then you are flirting with me. Is this your way of asking me out? I know I can be irresistible, and you seem quite taken with me. You know you are very attractive yourself," I said.

"You are kind of cute, but I don't think you are really my type," Maria said, pulling away and beginning to walk back toward her styling chair.

"Kind of cute? What does that even mean? I am cute! You are too! I think we should decide how to meet outside of this work environment," I exclaimed. She did not look back.

"I am off duty when you are off. I am single and certainly I am looking to explore new opportunities," she said. By this time, Maria was back at her station. During the shift she walked up and down the aisle behind each of the stylists. Just before the shift ended, and there were just the two of us left in the salon, Maria came over to me again.

"I am about to leave. If you find me interesting and you want to see me, here is my address. I will be home, changed, and waiting for you in twenty-five minutes. I live only about five minutes from here. I am worth a visit," she said, handing me a note and walking away. "I know Mrs. Hanson gave you a key for your Sunday work. Please use it to lock-up tonight.

"I think you are older than I. How do you feel about dating a younger guy?" I asked.

"I am wiser because of my age. I am more set in my ways. I am prettier. I can teach you a lot. Don't be late," she cautioned. As Maria walked away, she let her hair, which had been pulled up in a French twist, fall down cascading into a shoulder length flowing style. Her professional walk and demeanor suddenly became less rigid and a movement that can only be described as sexy replaced it. There was a new, energetic, almost fashion model type of walk taking place. As she exited the salon, she gave one last quick half-turn and waved good-bye. I knew it would be only a short time, about twenty minutes, between then and the next time we would see each other. I looked at my hand and opened her note so I could see the address. I saw that she lived on Memory Lane. I hoped it was a sign of good things to come.

I quickly put all my supplies away, swept up the hair around my styling booth, and made my area clean and ready for the next day. When I went back to the shampoo area, I noticed a small bouquet of flowers a client had given me earlier that day. I took out two of the roses and placed them in a wet paper towel to take to Maria. I turned off the lights to the salon and locked the door. I got to my car and looked again at the note. Turning it over, I saw that Maria had drawn a map from the salon to her house on that side. I started my car and decided to begin a new journey.

When I arrived at her apartment, I saw that she lived in a four-plex and that her unit was upstairs. There was only one unit that had lights on, and it was the one on the upper right side of the building. I parked my car, picked up the two roses from the other seat, looked at the front mirror to make sure my hair was combed and in place, smiled, and stepped out of the car to have my first date with Maria.

I knocked on the front door. When the door opened, I saw a beautiful woman standing in front of me. She was wearing a black dress that was cut so low that the tops of her breasts were showing and was short at the bottom to expose her long slender legs. She was wearing high heels that matched the color of her dress. Of course, her hair was expertly styled. She looked like a photo on the cover of a fashion magazine that had been airbrushed to make the model appear without blemish. For just a second, I tried to take in the room behind her. I could tell it was the living room, and I noticed there were many candles behind her, producing a very romantic glow. Soft music could be heard.

"I've been waiting for you, Ronnie," she said. I never heard anyone call me Ronnie. I was either Ron or Ronald. I started to correct her when she said it again. "What took you so long to show-up Ronnie?" This time she put an extra emphasis on the "ie" sound that made it really sound like "Ron EE" and showed that she had a Spanish accent, that I had not noticed at work.

"Did you just call me Ronnie?" I asked.

"Yes, don't you think it is sexy?" she said, opening the screen door and pulling me into the room. Both the screen door and the main door to the house were then closed. Now I was able to identify the music; it was Diana Ross singing "Ain't No Mountain High Enough." She pulled me toward her and placed her hands behind my head and drew me close. She established eye contact and I felt she was looking at my very soul. She smiled and I noticed that her teeth were perfect. As she pulled me tighter, I felt one of her legs circling and touching the backside of one of my legs like you would see performed in a tango. She kissed me. At first it was just a brush of our lips, then there was a short retreat and a much firmer kiss that spread over my entire mouth. Suddenly I felt her tongue enter my mouth. It was the first time I had ever experienced a French kiss and it was not from a French woman. It was from a Latina woman, who knew exactly what she wanted. She was now expertly moving my body in tune with the directions she wanted me to move. Her hands were rubbing up and down my body. She was pressing against me, making a sound I had not heard before.

Suddenly she stopped. She took my hands and pulled me toward the sofa. "Ronnie, I told you I could teach you many things. What do you think so far?" she asked.

"I think you are earning a passing grade. I haven't given you an "A" yet, but you are better than a "B," which means you are certainly above average," I joked, smiling as largely as possible so she would know I was kidding and that I was completely satisfied with her performance so far.

"If this were school, I would be satisfied with a "B," but I know I am a perfect "A" student in this subject matter," she said as she directed me to sit on the sofa next to her. She let go of my hand and took her hand and rubbed it up my leg. As she touched the top of my leg, she suddenly moved closer to the coffee table and took two glasses from it. She offered one of them to me.

"Let us toast our new relationship. I think it best to keep it a secret so none of the people at work will know. I don't want them to think I am giving you special treatment; because at work, I won't. But here, you may earn some extra credit, Ronnie," she said. We spent the next few hours learning about each other both intellectually and physically. I learned that her parents, like mine, had come to California as itinerant farm laborers. She was born here so she was a citizen and had made it out of the fields by becoming a cosmetologist. She lived on her own but felt it was time she settled down and found a husband. She had given herself a timeframe that only had a few months left before she wanted to be married. I also learned that she could make any man happy in certain ways. I, however, did not know if I could be that special person she wanted.

I had a social and educational event with the forensics team scheduled for the next evening. It was an evening when several students would be asked to perform their competitive program before everyone else and be critiqued by the entire group. Our graduate assistant, Susan, had arranged for about ten of us to come and learn together. She had told us we could bring a date so it would be a social event as well as a practice session. It was a potluck and was being held in the amphitheater behind the squad room on campus. I asked Maria if she would like to attend with me as my date.

"If it is a party, I think that would be fun. Should we bring food and some type of wine or beer?" she asked.

"I don't think beer or wine would be a good idea. It is at the college and it will be with other team members, many of whom are underage. It is a good time for you to meet some of my new friends," I told her.

"I have not gone to college, Ronnie, so what do I say to them?" she asked.

"Simply say you that are my girlfriend and that you are the manager of the hair salon where I work. They will be impressed about your job and how beautiful a person you are," I responded. I did not leave her home until about 1:00 a.m.

The next day I picked up Maria a half hour before the practice social was to start. She looked beautiful. She was wearing a pantsuit that combined high fashion and style. The high heels she had chosen to wear made her about four inches taller, but they also made her legs about four inches longer. Any man would have been proud to introduce her as his date. I noticed something different about her. Tonight, she was wearing glasses; they were not sunglasses. They were round framed glasses that were red rimmed.

"I didn't know you wore glasses. Those are great. You look like you could be an attorney," I said.

"I usually wear my contacts, but I thought if we are going to be with your college friends, I should look intelligent," she confided.

"You look wonderful. You don't have to try to impress this group. They will accept you as you are. You are a successful and beautiful person. Be proud of yourself and your accomplishments. Besides, you don't look your age and none of these people will know you have robbed the cradle because most of them don't know how old anyone else is and they don't really care about age," I teased. I knew she was approaching thirty and she felt that milestone would change her life.

"It is easy for you to say because you don't have any deadlines closing in on you, Ronnie," she observed.

"I do have deadlines. I must get through college as quickly as possible because I am paying for it myself with the assistance of some loans, grants, and scholarships. I want to be teaching in high school or college by the time I am twenty-four at the latest.

"But what about marriage? Do you want to get married?" she asked.

"Of course, some day. If two people are together in a solid relationship, the marriage certificate is a piece of paper that says they have decided to commit to each other for life. I know I am not ready to do that at this point. Let's go and enjoy our second date," I said.

We went to the social practice. The other students were very hospitable. As I expected, the guys were very impressed with Maria. Truthfully, she was the prettiest woman in attendance. The girls on the team were very friendly toward her. It was the first time Maria had seen the various programs like dramatic interpretation, humorous interpretation, and program reading. She had never been to a speech competition and had never heard an informative or persuasive speech before. She held onto my hand and appeared to be having a good time. By the end of the evening, I could tell she was ready to go. I knew the practice session had really helped those of us participating. Maria had whispered to me, after I had performed, that she thought I had done the best and was glad she was with me. When we got back to her place, we had the following conversation: "I liked your friends. They seemed nice, but I don't think I would like to be around them a lot," Maria said.

"What makes you say that?"

"There were many things they said that I did not understand. I felt like I was back in school and had to work at trying to be a part of everything. At the salon I am the expert and we talk about common things like birthdays, anniversaries, vacations, children, things that are going on in life; but we don't talk about intellectual, political, or things we can't control," she said.

"My friends will not try to dominate their conversations with you. Besides, we would not see them much except for social functions. That was a practice session; I don't even know if there will be any more of those this semester. If you don't want to go, I can go alone. People will accept you if they accept me. I am not ashamed of you and you should have confidence that you are a person just as knowledgeable as anyone else," I said.

"Ronnie, you are so sweet and caring. I have my life planned out and I must be married by my thirtieth birthday. Do you think you could be my husband?" she asked.

"I cannot see myself being married without having finished my education," I responded.

"Between the two of us, we can make a very comfortable living doing hair," she predicted.

"I don't want to do hair for the rest of my life. I have always wanted to put myself through college, so I don't have to work in the fields, pump gas, or be a sales associate. Doing hair has always been a way to get away from one point in my life and get onto the next. I am not going to college to end up styling hair."

"But, Ronnie, you are so good at it, and you are already charging more than anyone I know for your haircuts; and the clients, both men and women, already love you," Maria said, trying to convince me to continue styling hair.

"I have always wanted to go to college, complete it, and then teach at some level. We have to accomplish our own goals," I said.

"My goal is to be financially secure enough to have my own place to live, have a car that is nice, buy the things I want, and be able to go on vacations from time to time. I have these goals and with both of us working, we can succeed," she claimed.

"I want to be able to buy a home, have a new car every two or three years, visit many places on vacation, and enjoy life in every aspect. I don't doubt that we could open our own salon and become wealthy enough to accomplish these things; but I don't want to do it with styling hair as my profession. If you are willing to wait until I graduate, I think we have a chance of being together, but I am just getting to know you," I confessed.

"What if we marry and you continue to go to college and do hair here in Fresno. We can open our own salon and I can run it for us. I already have a name I would like to use. "The Hair Affair" would be a great name and we could run it together. What do you think, Ronnie?" she asked.

"If we open our own salon, there will be much more stress and demand on both of us to make sure it succeeds. The first couple of years I would have to devote much more time than just showing up and doing my own thing several times a week. I am not ready. I don't think I can do both. I must finish college. I would consider us having our own salon once I started teaching and know I have a stable income that can sustain us through the early stages of owning a business. We can start saving and working together. We can move in together and begin saving and planning for the future," I suggested.

"I don't think that is possible, Ronnie. I must meet my objectives too!" she said, beginning to cry.

"I am not saying we can't be together. We can even discuss marriage. I just can't commit to it within the next several months," I tried to clarify.

"My deadline, my birthday, is not several months from now. It is only next month," Maria declared.

"I cannot meet that time deadline," I told her.

"Then we need to break up. I love you but I will have to find a substitute," she said. As she finished these words, she closed the door to her apartment. I stood alone on the steps leading from her front door.

Two Saturdays later as we were closing the salon, the door opened and an older gentleman, about fifty, entered. He smiled at Maria. "Hi, Honey," he said to her. He walked over toward her, and they kissed. She took hold of his hand and they walked toward me.

"Raymond, this is Ron; Ron this is Raymond, my fiancée. I have told Raymond about what a great a hair stylist you are and how happy we are to have you as part of our team here at the salon because you make all of us perform at a higher level," she said, trying to cover-up the real reason why he was here.

"Raymond, nice to meet you. What brings you here to the salon? Is Maria going to cut your hair or are you two planning to hold a wedding here at the salon? That would be a different affair. I didn't even know Maria was seeing anyone," I said, trying to gain additional information from Raymond.

"No, we are not here for that. We met last Sunday at a nearby laundromat. We have seen each other every night since. I popped the question last night and Maria said she wants to get married next weekend because that will make her dream of being married by the time, she is thirty, come true. It will certainly make my dream come true, to be with someone as pretty and bright as she is," he said.

"Do you have a deadline for getting married too?" I asked.

"No. This will be my third and final marriage. I have never been so lucky, nor have I learned so much about pleasing a woman as I have in the last week," he said with a huge smile.

"I know what you mean. I once was lucky like you. I found a woman, very similar to Maria, who taught me many things, but I let her get away. I wish you the best and you know you have made the best decision regarding a woman you could make. Good luck to both of you. Sorry we can't talk more now, but I have to get to an appointment, and I am already late. See you, Maria. I am happy for both of you. They say that when two people meet and are meant to be together, sometimes you just know it and should act on it immediately," I added, as I walked out the door knowing I had made the right decision, not to marry Maria.

Six months later Maria announced she was pregnant. Just before the baby was born, she told us that Raymond had left her, and she was facing motherhood by herself.

Maria had wanted to marry someone desperately. Though I was almost ten years younger than she, she saw me as the right man at the right time. Did she love me? I will never know. We had only two real dates. I do know that fifty years later she was still the most beautiful obstacle to my career goals I ever met. In the next chapter you will meet three other women who greatly affected my life.

CHAPTER SIXTEEN

In addition to my experience with Maria, three other encounters with older women must be mentioned. All of them took place during my first year at "Fashions by Hazel" and all of them left me unhappy and alone. Each one presented me with a personal obstacle I would have to overcome.

From the beginning, Mrs. Hanson's strategy had been to ask more for my services than any other stylist in the Fresno area was receiving. She thought I could get away with this because I was one of the very few males doing women's hair at the time and because my clients seemed quite pleased with my work. This strategy had an additional benefit for me because having higher prices meant I needed fewer clients and would have more time to spend on my college courses and forensics competitions.

On the other hand, having fewer clients meant that I had to do everything I could to hold on to each of them. To my pleasant surprise, there was no shortage of people willing to spend what I was asking, if only to brag to their friends how much they were spending to get their hair done right. I charged twenty-five dollars for a haircut. Most cuts consisted of taking longer hair and making it considerably shorter either by cutting it with scissors (a time consuming procedure) or for those clients wanting to keep their long hair but needing the split ends cut, I would light a candle and burn off damaged or unruly hair; taking care, of course, not to burn healthy hair. While the fire technique did a better job of eliminating split ends than using scissors to cut the frayed ends, it produced an unpleasant odor. Nevertheless, I charged an extra fifty dollars for this treatment.

Three women were so pleased by my efforts, they considered me a new best friend and confidant. They all requested me to go to their residences for one-on-one sessions. I informed them there would be an extra fifty-dollar charge for travel time, but they all agreed to meet my price. I had to keep them happy.

Delaney was a Caucasian woman, about fifty-five years old, who worked for the fire department as a 911 dispatcher. For the past eight years she had also been a student at Fresno State, where she was now a senior, majoring in social work.

One Saturday we were just finishing up at the salon when she told me it was taking her longer than most students to graduate from college because she had difficulty writing academic papers, which have stylistic, editing, and footnote requirements. She asked me what I might charge to edit her work for her. I told her my fee would be thirty dollars per hour. She did not blink. The next week she gave me a paper she had been working on for some time. "I don't really know what I am doing, but I have tried to outline my position and develop a thesis statement," she explained.

I told her I would edit her work, but she had to write the paper. "You are a psychiatric social work major. I am sure the professor has given you and your classmates a very specific assignment. I need to know what that was before we get started," I added.

"After a while, the assignments all sound the same to me," she yawned as she spoke. I thought that, perhaps, she had been up late struggling with her assignment.

"Explain to me in your own words what you want to say and what you will use to support that position," I requested.

"I was hoping you would do this for me. I really need your help," she said. "My professor wants me to explain why certain people act on an impulse to do something they know is breaking the law and why others will not," she said. For the first time I felt she knew what she was being asked to do and understood what needed to be developed. "She also expects us to interview some people," she added.

"Why do you think some act out while others do not?" I asked.

She thought about this for a few seconds before answering, "I think some people respect the laws that govern our society while others feel they can make up rules of their own or think they do not have to obey rules that they don't like." She spoke in a voice that got softer as she came to the end of the sentence. Then she looked away, refusing to look me in the eyes.

"I like that response. I think we can use it as a basis for your paper's position," I said in an affirming manner.

"Really?" Suddenly she had a smile on her face, and she exhibited much more confidence.

"I knew you could help me."

"Yes, I think you can develop a logical and defensible position," I declared.

"I wish I had met you eight years ago," she responded in a lighthearted manner and a big smile accompanied the statement.

"Eight years ago, I was still in junior high school," I replied.

She thought for a minute longer. "I am a good cook. Would you like to come to dinner and then we could work on my paper some Friday or Saturday evening?" she suggested. "I live alone, so no one will bother us," she added.

"I usually have people drop off their assignments to me and then I call or meet them in a library setting," I explained.

"I am not your average person. I can make it worth your while. I have many more papers for you to help me with so I can get me my degree. Once I complete the degree, I will get a huge raise in my salary. I want to get the increase before I retire and then it will help me get a much better retirement, since my retirement is based on my final year's salary."

"What do you want me to do? Just show up?" I asked.

"Show up with an appetite and plan to stay a while. I have a pool and it is enclosed and heated to just the right temperature," she said with a smile.

"I don't know about swimming right after eating," I teased.

"I didn't say swimming would come right after dinner. There might be some time for swimming after eating and working on my paper," she said, as she passed me a piece of paper with her address on it.

"I have a pretty tight schedule," I reminded her.

"Just work me in when you can. Money spent for my education is no problem," she said. By this time, I had finished styling her hair; and she was reaching for her money. After she paid me, she made it a point to count out my tip aloud. "Five, ten, fifteen, twenty, twenty-five dollars; and there is plenty more waiting for you," she whispered.

"This is a very nice tip," I said smiling at her. She too was smiling. She appeared to be in a very good mood. She had a confidence about herself that she had not displayed before.

"I can't wait for you to try my cooking and to enjoy my pool," she said. "Call me the day before you can come. You won't regret it," she said as she walked away from my station.

I thought a great deal about how to handle this situation. After reading her essay, I knew she needed a lot of help with editing and grammar, redirection in how she developed some of her ideas, and help with her choice of words. Overall, however, her work was accurate, supported, and personal. She needed someone to edit the small errors, which added together resulted in a paper that was average at best, depending on the quality of work of the other students in her class. At least that is what I told myself when I agreed to help her.

It was ten days before I called her. I met her at her home. My plan was to keep the meeting very professional and to avoid at all costs any type of personal contact that would imply something more than a desire to help her with her paper. Her home was a nice one-story ranch style with a large front yard with trees on both sides and a well-manicured lawn. By any standard it was an upscale home in a very impressive neighborhood. I was right on time for our appointment and I rang the doorbell. I could see her in the living room, but she did not appear in any hurry to open the door. I rang the doorbell again. This time she opened the main door but kept the screen door closed.

"I will open the screen in just a minute," she said as I waited outside. Finally, she opened the screen but stood between me and the open entry way.

"Sorry, but it is not often I get a handsome man at my door. My nosy neighbors are looking at us right now and soon they will be on their phones telling others what they have seen. Do you mind if we stay out here just a minute or two longer? I want to give all of them a good look at you and ample time to think about it," she admitted.

I noticed right away that she was wearing a very pretty dress, an expensive looking necklace, and had on very high heeled shoes. She had obviously gone to great lengths to look as good as possible for me.

"My neighbors do not understand that I try to meet men, but so far I have not met the one who wants to accept me as I am. I have given up trying; well at least most of the time. I don't think dating is in my immediate future. It hurts when these people I live near and who really care about me, don't understand nor accept my position," she shared.

I thought about the times I felt alone, especially when I felt inferior to others. Luckily, I had been given confidence and reassurance by teachers and ministers. She had not met the right people, who could recognize her strengths and abilities. As she finally allowed me to enter, I could not resist the temptation to help her out by giving the neighbors something more to talk about.

"Are you sure they are all looking?" I asked.

"Oh, they are watching us. A few of them even have binoculars. Some worry about me; but most feel sorry for me because I have not met a man who wants me."

"Well, let's make the night worthwhile for all the spectators. I hope you won't mind what I am about to do," I declared. I stepped back from the screen and motioned for Delaney to come out onto the front of the porch so that no one would miss what was about to happen. I pulled her close and pretended to give her a kiss that lasted for fifteen seconds. I know it did because I counted them. Delaney looked startled at first, but quickly gave way to this impromptu gesture. She then took me by the hand and led me into the house. Once we were inside, the drapes were closed and dinner and work on her paper proceeded without any type of physical contact. Throughout the evening I kept telling her that she was in control of her own destiny and that her decision to get a college degree was something that few others could claim. She insisted that we swim, so I got into the pool with her. Several times she tried to hug me, but I politely moved away from her. Over the next few months, I helped her with six different papers and found myself doing more and more of the writing. At graduation she was recognized for her accomplishments and for her endurance. She received a raise at work and was able to retire a few years later with, I assume, much better pay. Once the last paper had been completed, however, I never heard from her again. In spite of all I had done for her I lost her as a client.

* * * * *

Not long afterwards, I met Shirley who was about forty years old and a recent divorcee. Her hair reached a good five inches below her shoulders. I had colored her dull blonde hair with three lighter shades of blond and two shades of light brown, but it still lacked something. I decided it was time for me to shorten her hair.

"You know I completely trust your judgement as to how I should wear my hair," she said, looking into the mirrored wall in front of us.

"I know you should trust me," I said with more than a little pride.

"I do. I think it is time for me to change my persona."

"I am the one to do just that for you. Let's take your hair short. You will look like you are thirty or younger when I am finished," I promised her jokingly. I did not really think she would look like someone in her twenties.

"I turn myself over to your hands," she declared. "A new look might be just what is needed to get me back in the dating scene."

"I don't think you will be disappointed. You will certainly make that ex-husband of yours think twice about why he let you get away," I predicted. I did not want her to back out of her decision because I knew one thing for sure; she would look amazing when I finished her cut and style.

"Let's do this!" she agreed.

"Yes, my lady," I said as I bowed at the waist. I pulled her hair back behind her head. I took my scissors and cut off most of what I held. I showed her how much hair I had in my hand and how long it was. She gasped.

"What have you done?" she asked in a loud voice.

"You just contributed to help children who have lost their hair due to cancer. I will be sending these locks of hair to have wigs made for two small children. I will tell the recipients who donated the hair and you will receive thank you letters from them. But the real blessing is in knowing you have helped children who will now be able to look into a mirror and no longer see bald heads," I said, while taking out a bag to hold her hair so we could send it to help those who had a special need for it. "Hair Care for Kids" would soon be making another child with cancer, who had lost their hair, feel better.

"But look at me now. I guess it is too late to back out." She was almost in tears.

"Don't worry. Let's go back to the shampoo bowl so I can wash your hair and give you a wet cut that will offer us many possibilities."

We walked to the shampoo room, which was uncharacteristically vacant, and sat her down at bowl three in the middle of the room. She reclined in her seat. As I began to wash her hair, she allowed her elbow to brush up against my pant leg. I looked down at her. Most women, who do what she did, have their eyes open so they can see what type of reaction I give them. Her eyes were closed so my first thought was that her movement had been accidental. I was wrong. Suddenly, her hand was rubbing up and down my leg. I moved further away from the bowl so that she could no longer reach me. I turned off the water, gently raised her head up from the sink, and pushed her chair up from a reclining position to a sitting up one.

"You are going to look amazing," I said, as I began to massage her shoulders, as I did with every client whom I shampooed. There is just something about having your shoulders massaged after having your hair washed that makes you feel relaxed. We started walking back to my styling chair. By the time I had performed my magic there, she looked younger, perky, and sophisticated. No one who saw her for the first time would ever believe she was forty. She loved her new look.

"Is there anything I can do for you to repay you for this transformation?" she asked, as she stood up to pay for cutting, coloring, and styling of her hair.

"You already did the right thing by allowing us to use your hair for the "Hair Care for Kids" program; but as you know, my services do not come free. Tonight, you owe $125." She handed me two one hundred-dollar bills. I started to get her change, but she stopped me.

"Don't bother with change. This night has been worth every penny of $200," she said, walking out of the salon looking at least ten years younger than she had when she entered. She had a great haircut and some fun with me as well, I told myself it had been worth it, but deep down I was beginning to wonder if I were willing to do too much to keep a client happy.

* * * * *

Most of my tips, like Shirley's, came in the form of cash. I will never forget one that did not. It came from Brenda, a cocktail waitress at one of the busiest restaurants on Blackstone Avenue in the evening and the manager of a hotel nearby during the day. She told me that she never worked fewer than seventy hours per week. I guessed that she was in her late sixties. I was not surprised that she sometimes came to her appointment with me tired, sleepy, and slightly cranky. At other times she displayed energy, spunk, and an outgoing personality that made her seem quite a bit younger.

"Do you know why I come to you every week?" she asked me once.

"Because you want the best stylist in Fresno to do your hair," I replied.

"You are the first person who has ever done my hair so well that it lasts the entire week," she said, as I brushed the very stiff and teased hair, which apparently had not been touched for a week. I did not say so, but I thought it nearly impossible for someone to go an entire week without washing his or her hair, but I did not want to alienate her.

Brenda would arrive for her appointment and leave looking almost exactly the same way she did when she came in. It took five minutes for me to comb all the teasing out of her long hair that she wanted styled in a French twist with large barrel curls. I would then shampoo her hair with a special product for over-processed and colored hair. I next used a conditioner to untangle her hair and make it free of any teased strands. She liked the fact that I allowed her to remain in a reclined fashion at the shampoo bowl for fifteen minutes or so while I worked on another client. I always made sure to give Brenda a three-minute shoulder massage. She said she was grateful for it. After the massage I set her hair in large rollers to give her maximum straightness with only a slight resemblance of curl after it had dried. She insisted that I put her under the dryer for at least one hour. She claimed this was the best sleep she got all week. When it was time for her to come out of the dryer, she would ask other clients if they wanted to go ahead of her and allow her to remain under the dryer for a longer time. If someone agreed, I turned the temperature of her dryer down from hot to cold, cooling her hair and scalp. Once she remained under the dryer for three consecutive hours. She loved to sleep at the salon; she never wanted to leave. One Saturday, when she was my last client of the day, she spent the entire afternoon asleep under the dryer.

"OK, Brenda, you have to wake-up now; we need to finish making you ready to face your public for another week," I said.

"If I could have just fifteen more minutes, that would be great," she pleaded, looking up at me with one eye still closed.

"You have allowed everyone else to go ahead of you. It takes exactly ten minutes to comb your hair and about five minutes for me to spray a can of hair spray, so your hair does not move," I reminded her.

"You can complete all of your cleaning up before you comb my hair," she insisted, knowing what I had to do before closing for the night.

"I will let you have the time it takes for me to clean my combs and brushes, sweep the floor, and put the towels I have used in the dirty hamper. That is all the time you get," I said in a somewhat authoritarian voice that she knew I did not really mean.

"You really need to come by the lounge some night so I can start to repay you for all you do for me," she said.

"If I come by, are you going to give me free drinks?" I asked, somewhat hopefully.

"I was thinking of something free; but it wasn't drinks. Most of the girls, who work there at night, work for me during the day at the hotel in the front office or in housekeeping. I am sure you could find one of them to be attractive to you," she said confidently. Brenda and I had never had a conversation like this before.

"Brenda, you sound like you might be a madam or have some other illegal occupation." I must admit that I was very curious to find out exactly what she was offering me.

"I don't take a share of what any of them do at night so that relieves me from ever being considered a madam. I do give them reduced rates for the rooms at the hotel they use and they in turn offer me very generous tips," she explained, smiling, no doubt, at my shocked facial expression upon learning she had a secret life.

"Do you worry about the law, or about being arrested, or what might happen to you if any of your girls get caught?" I asked.

"Look at me. Do you think that anyone is going to care how someone my age meets their financial obligations? Besides, many of my most active clients are police, district attorneys, public defenders, judges, and undercover vice. None of them are going to say anything about me or my day and night jobs because I can reveal what I know about them just as loudly. They all have more to lose than I do," she bragged. As she was speaking, she pushed the dryer up and walked over to the chair where I would do the best I could to make her hair beautiful for another week.

"If I were to show up at the lounge some evening, and I am not saying I will, what could you do that might protect me from being caught up in a raid or some kind of sting operation," I wondered.

"You would be my guest and that assures you the ultimate protection from those who are opposed to what I am providing," she promised.

About a month later I found myself pulling into the lounge on Blackstone, where Brenda was working as usual. As I entered, I felt a fascinating drive of energy from the music, a beat I had not heard in the few bars and lounges I had visited before. Brenda motioned me to join her at the bar, where she was obviously holding court.

"I see you finally decided to visit us. What brings you here tonight?" she asked.

"I was ditched by a friend tonight. We had an argument and I am feeling depressed. I could use some friendly companionship. Although one person doesn't want me; maybe someone else will," I said, articulating my hopes for the rest of the evening.

"I am sure we can make the rest of your night more delightful than it was earlier," Brenda said, making a motion with her arm that a conductor might make just as the orchestra begins. Four beautiful women rushed over to her, waiting for instructions.

"Girls, this is my friend Ron. I want him to have a night he will never forget. You will find him creative, gentle, and kind. He is my guest and nothing but the best is good enough for him. Is that understood?" she asked those huddled around us.

I took just a minute to examine each of the women. One was blonde, one a brunette, one Asian, and one black. As I was looking them over, Brenda handed me a drink.

"Start your evening with our newest drink, a Long Island Iced Tea," she said handing me a tall glass. I took the drink, which I thought held iced tea. I thanked her and, being very thirsty, I drank it down quickly. It was slightly sweet and had a strong flavor I had never gotten from iced tea before. I thought I would have to ask later what brand of tea they were using. I really liked it.

"Brenda, how am I supposed to choose from four such beautiful women?" I asked.

"You don't have to choose one. This is my treat. Choose two or even all four of them. They can work as a team to make sure you are satisfied," Brenda assured me. She handed me another tea. I drank it with a few large swallows. My heart was beating slowly, and I felt my body letting the stress and anger I had experienced earlier that evening begin to dissipate.

To this point in my life I had been drunk only once, when I was doing an assignment for a class on the effects of beer drinking. Now I felt light-headed, but another tea was handed to me. It was still the best tea I had ever tasted; smooth, sweet, and very refreshing. I don't know what came over me, but I started to laugh at the situation. I had four beautiful women vying for my attention. As I finished my drink, one of the women was kissing my ears; another was massaging my shoulders; the third was rubbing my mid-section; and the last was massaging my thighs. I was seated but I don't remember sitting down. I heard one of the women say to Brenda, "I don't think he is much of a drinker."

"Girls, your job is to make him happy. Give him this last drink and then take him across the street to room 640 and do what you do best," Brenda told them, leaving me in their capable hands as she went to take care of someone else. I drank one last iced tea and all four of the women helped me out of the bar and we stumbled across the street toward the hotel and took the elevator to room 640.

I do not remember anything that happened after that. We must have made it to the right room, and I may have had the time of my life, but I have no memory of it. All I know for sure is that I woke up the next morning about 10:00 a.m. I was in bed alone, and my clothes had been dumped on a nearby chair.

Until now I have never discussed this evening with anyone, not even with Brenda. Sometime later I learned that a Long Island Iced Tea contains equal parts of vodka, gin, tequila, rum, and a touch of coke which gives it the color of traditional iced tea. I am sure I could have accepted the free drinks and called a cab without hurting Brenda's feelings, but once again I did not want to offend her, and I allowed myself to drink to excess. I was becoming someone I did not want to be.

CHAPTER SEVENTEEN

To someone observing my life from afar, it undoubtedly appeared to be going much better than they would have predicted. I was in my second semester at Fresno State, had met some really nice students I called friends, was taking enough units to allow me not only to complete my B.A. degree in three semesters, but would also allow me to complete the first six units toward an M.A. degree within four semesters of attending Fresno State. I had established a hair styling business at "Hair Fashions by Hazel" that was lucrative and flexible in scheduling to accommodate classes and tournaments, and offered me loyal clients, who allowed me to style their hair in the way I thought best. But these observations were from the outside.

From my own perspective, my life was quite different. My feelings bordered on depression. I found myself struggling with my relationship with God, with church attendance, with personal insecurity, and loneliness. From the time I had entered high school, there wasn't a move I made that did not have something to do with my planning and putting into action a plan that would allow me to get out of the agricultural fields. I had my mother, teachers, ministers, and friends to help and encourage me. Now I felt alone even while being surrounded by people.

I was experimenting with heavy drinking, dating women quite a bit older than myself, pretending to have feelings for them that I really did not have, and constantly seeking approval from my professors and coaches. At least I hoped I could learn enough to become a successful debate coach.

Debating well takes time and, unfortunately, that commodity was something I did not have. Most great debaters start in high school and continue to develop in college with the help of expert coaching and few distractions. I had only this inaugural year and the next one to learn all that I could before graduation. My debate partner and I made great progress because of the help and role modeling of our senior debaters, who were willing not only to debate us but would critique us and help us learn to structure arguments. Inside our own squad we were called the "Cocky Novice Team" because we felt we were better than any other teams that were new to the activity. What we did not understand until we were debating in some of the elimination rounds was that coaches from other schools allowed their students, regardless of years of experience, to compete in novice division until they had won a tournament. Our opponents often had four years more debating experience than we did.

We had, however, one great advantage. Our top team, Don Morley and Michael Weatherson, was willing to help us and was instrumental in our rapid rise in the novice debate world. Perhaps our greatest learning experience came when we got to observe them debating in senior division elimination rounds. We learned how they responded to each other, how they reacted to their opponents, and how they interacted with the audience. We also saw the stylistic differences that made them better than most other teams. We paid special attention to how they asked questions during cross examination, how they challenged various pieces of evidence used by the opposition, and how they always appeared to be in control of the situation.

One of the most memorable teaching moments came when they were debating in an elimination round against one of the best teams in the country at a tournament in Reno, Nevada. The debate was held in a theatre at the campus and was filled with spectators who seemed to be equally divided in support for each team. Before the round started, I wished Don and Mike good luck. Morley responded, "Luck will have no part in this round. We have prepared for this debate all season, and if we execute what we have been taught by Bochin, and if my colleague Mike mitigates the affirmative's need issues, I, with my analysis, impeccable evidence, charm, and personality will force the judges to vote for us." He looked directly at me and continued: "That is the part you and Kathy have to work on to become better than novice stars. We can help you with the arguments but you must learn to clarify them to the highest level so they can be understood by the smart judges, by the not so smart ones, and even by the dumb ones. Just sit back now and watch us!" he said.

Kathy and I watched closely. After each speaker, the audience was convinced that speaker was telling the truth, was honest and persuasive; but most importantly, was the person you wanted to be the winner. The last speaker for our team during the rebuttals was Don. The timer indicated he had only thirty seconds before his rebuttal speech would begin and started a countdown. Don was preparing notes for himself.

The timer spoke: "Five, four, three, two, one; your time begins," she said. I was very concerned and frightened. We almost never had enough time to get through all the arguments during this last speech, and Don was giving time away. I would be panicking if it were happening to me. Don just sat there finishing his notes. He looked up to the audience and said to the timer:

"Please feel free to take off any time I have used up to this point. I won't need all of it to do my job." I was watching the timer and now only three of Don's four minutes were left. Finally, Don rose, started his speech, and masterfully reviewed all of Mike's case arguments and pointed out two huge disadvantages that would hurt society if the plan of action advocated by the affirmative team were adopted.

As Don finished, Mike rose to his feet and went to shake his hand. At the same time, the entire audience gave Don a standing ovation. Audience members supporting both teams recognized what a superb job he had done. In that very minute I realized that the art of competitive debate is about seeking and finding the strengths and weaknesses of both sides of an issue and crystalizing your own arguments and making them understandable so that the listener has to agree with your position.

Kathy and I quickly rose from the novice level and became very competitive at the junior level. We even did well in one senior level division tournament by the end of the academic year. Neither of us had the time, nor were we willing to put our other goals aside, to become elite senior level debaters the following year. The senior participants on our team contributed to our success and allowed us to accomplish much more than we novice speakers would have been able to do at any other college. We gained much from them and helped the team to earn more sweepstake trophies that year than ever had been earned previously. Their constant nurturing, critiquing, and being solid role models made our debate experience and journey from novice to senior division within the academic year a success that proved to me I was capable and, with help, could overcome my lack of experience.

Both Morley and Weatherson went on to become college professors. Their colleges, students, and the communities in which they lived, taught, and shared their talents were benefited by their presence. It was a pleasure for me to have been under their tutelage because I became a better person and debater because of them. I never rose to their level, but because of them and Dr. Bochin, I was able to assist my students in finding the highest level within themselves. I had been taught the fundamental job of coaching, which is to support, to educate, and to practice. Some of my students far exceeded my accomplishments and I am happy to give credit to them for any debate awards my students earned.

* * * * *

I had no choice but to work while attending college. Hair styling became a means for me to succeed financially during my upper division and graduate years; but it also provided a challenging obstacle in many ways because of the people I met, who demanded more than styling services from me. I found myself fashioning the hair of many older women, who proved themselves to be quite difficult at times. Some wanted personal favors I could not or would not provide. At one point I considered just walking away from styling hair because I felt it was having a detrimental effect on my education and psyche. I found myself having to be on call at any time there was a hair "emergency" and I was being given more and more appointments each day I was working because clients, who were having their hair done by some of the other stylists, saw my work and begged the owner for an appointment with me.

It became very stressful even to find the energy to go to work. I remembered a time when I did hair for fun. I had loved doing Momma's hair and my sister Nellie's hair because it was a way to thank them for what they had done for me. I wanted to find an outlet that would restore the fun aspect of doing hair. Some hair cutting and styling became therapeutic when I styled some of the forensics members to repay them for their kindness and generosity. Of course, I never charged them the full price for my services.

One of my favorite memories of doing hair for fun took place when I helped one of the female debaters with her hair. I had met Michael and Patti on that first day when I arrived for my interview with Coach Bochin. I never imagined that they would play such an important role in my college years. Patti became a friend and a client of mine. She had long hair and she looked amazing when she had special occasions to prepare for and would come to the shop to have me style her hair.

Two incidents stand out as being special. The first took place before a New Year's Eve party. She and her sister came to the shop in the early afternoon. I shared with them that I was going to our company party that evening with a wide range of people, who would be attending, and I asked them if they were interested in being my guests. They reminded me of a party that some of the forensics team members were having that night as well. We decided we would attend both. My shop party was using the New York City time frame (three hours later than our time zone) and would end just a little after 9:00 p.m. our time. Our plans were to leave that party and go to the forensics one, which would have a younger crowd.

Once we got to the first party, we found ourselves the focal point of most of the guests because of our age, our youthful energy, and the fact we were attending Fresno State instead of some other college. Each of us had a great time drinking responsibly, enjoying many interpersonal encounters, making conversation with people from many walks of life, doing lots of dancing, as well as eating and singing. We never made it to the second party because we felt safe, content, and wanted at the staff party.

Another memorable moment took place a few years later before Patti's wedding. She asked me to style her hair for that special day and I agreed, as long as it would be my gift to her. To be a part of someone's wedding, especially for someone you know, respect, and care for, is a special event that lasts for a lifetime. The wedding pictures will always show how the bride looked that day. They will show how my hair styling added to Patti's beauty. Not many people will know or remember who did the styling. Patti, however, will remember and, hopefully, every time she looks at a wedding photograph, she will think of the stylist she encouraged to come to Fresno State and whom she helped get through his novice debating experiences. She joined my family as a surrogate sister.

* * * * *

When Momma was alive, she had kept me focused and supported my desire to get out of the fields. I wanted to make her proud of me. I found myself needing to have a talk with Momma. One Friday morning around 8:00 a.m. I got into my car after having spent an entire night crying. I had tried not to cry; but I had no control over it. I could not sleep; I was extremely depressed. Pulling off Highway 99 onto Laredo Highway, I saw the sign informing me that Shafter was seven miles away.

Those seven miles were the loneliest seven miles I have ever driven. I felt like all the desire I had to continue my life was gone. I had let down all those who had put their trust in me. I could not live up to their expectations. I saw the trees up ahead on the right side of the railroad tracks that circled the cemetery, where Momma was resting after her long and painful illness. She had lost her life before she should have. I remembered the tree that was the visual marker for where she was buried. As I pulled up to that tree, I remembered that she was located two burial plots from the curb. I took a deep breath and moved slowly toward her final resting place. None of those buried in this section of the cemetery had a tombstone, but I found her grave marker. It was about twelve inches long and four inches wide. Each side of the marker had round circular holes like one would find on a golf course. Instead of holes used to catch balls on a green, these holes were used to hold flowers. In Momma's case there were no flowers, no tombstone, no caring for the site. Weeds were growing on both sides of her marker. A pile of cut grass was stuck on the marker, covering over half of her full name. It appeared that no one had visited her site for quite a while. As I sat down on the ground beside her grave, I brushed away the grass that had been deposited from the lawn being mowed. I decided I could not have a conversation with Momma until I had cleaned up the site.

Soon I was in town at a hardware store where I bought a small broom, a pair of shears to cut the weeds, two bunches of flowers, one for each end of the marker, and a "Three Musketeers" candy bar; it was Momma's favorite. I paid for the supplies and returned to the cemetery.

The next thing I remember is sitting at Momma's grave. I had cut and pulled the weeds that had grown around the marker. I had put fresh colorful flowers into containers that fit into the holes at each end of the marker, swept off the name marker, and picked up the area. My visual inspection of the area found that most of the other sites had been as neglected as hers. I placed the "Three Musketeers" bar directly onto the name marker. It was time for us to talk.

"Momma, I am sorry I haven't been here sooner." I closed my eyes to see if I could imagine her near, see her, or find her by my side. When I opened my eyes, Momma was sitting in a rocking chair on the other side of the grave marker.

"I must say I thought you would come sooner than today, but what really matters is that you are here now," she said.

"For the first time, I think I have failed you and everyone else who believed in me. I feel so alone," I confessed.

"You are never alone. You have all the conversations we have had in the past to remember," she explained.

"What if I forget what you said?" I asked.

"You have a great memory. Take a couple of deep breaths and focus on a conversation in which we worked through an issue that was like the one which worries you today," she said.

"What will people think if I tell them I have conversations with my dead mother?" I asked.

"You don't have to tell anyone about our conversations. I did my best to give each of my children the help they would need to care for others and to make wise decisions. Our conversations have not disappeared. You have the power to recall and apply what I said. I always tried to choose my words to provide you with a means to make the right decisions," she said.

"Here I am, talking to a dead woman," I reiterated.

"I am not dead in your heart, am I?" she asked.

"Of course not. You will always be there. I have great memories of you," I shared.

"As long as you can remember me, you will never be alone. You don't even have to come here to talk with me," she said.

"I feel closer by being here," I quickly assured her.

"They placed my body here. I am not here; my soul has gone home to be with God," she claimed.

"I am having trouble finding a church to attend and knowing how to be a true Christian," I confessed.

"Remember, a church is only a building where people of like minds go to worship God. Your Christianity is not based on church attendance. Yet, as your mother, for what it is worth, I feel you have so much to offer. I think you are always a better person from going to church because people there help each other. Find a church that will accept you just as you are," she demanded.

"So many of them don't want their members to drink, or smoke, or divorce, or..." I tried to continue.

"Didn't Jesus serve wine to his disciples?" Momma interrupted.

"Yes, but..."

"Do you really think someone who smokes will be left out of heaven because of that?" she asked, smiling at the simplicity of that idea.

"No! There may be a smoking section somewhere in heaven," I admitted with a large smile.

"Do you think God wants people to live together if they are making each other unhappy? Divorce may be the answer for some," she suggested.

"You stayed with Father," I insisted.

"We did stay together. I never stopped loving your father. Did he have his faults? Of course, he did, but I wasn't perfect either," she tried to explain.

"You were pretty close," I said as quickly as possible.

"Had I not been so sick for so long, you would have learned some of my faults. Forgive your father," she insisted.

"I have forgiven him; I don't have to like him. He made his choices."

"What about yourself? Love others: but remember you cannot love others, without loving yourself," she said, reinforcing what she had shared with me so many times before.

"I love me; but right now, I don't like me very much," I whispered in disbelief of how low I had fallen in my own self-respect.

"If you do love yourself, then some action you have taken or are contemplating doing must be the reason why you do not like yourself. What have you done or are you considering doing that is causing this dislike?" she asked, trying to get to the core of the issue.

"I have not stood up for what I know to be true about how I really feel about certain women I have dated recently. They are generous to me with money, but I am only a means to a sexual result they want. I don't think they really care about me at all," I shared.

"You know the answer. Help them to the degree you can, but don't stay in a relationship just because it is easy for you or financially beneficial for you," she shared in her motherly fashion.

"I know. They are considerably older than I and they buy me nice things, but we are only using each other because I do not have much contact with women my own age. I meet many women at the beauty salon but most women my age cannot afford to have me do their hair. Most of the women in my classes, who interest me, already have someone," I said. "My job and my school activities take up all my weekends and that is prime dating time for most students," I continued.

"Don't make excuses. You need to be true to yourself. Take appropriate action," she insisted.

"I don't know what I am supposed to do. I don't know what anyone expects from me," I shared.

"What else is wrong?" she asked, moving her chair just enough to block the direct sunlight that was shining into my eyes. After she moved, I noticed she was wearing the same red dress we had bought for her that special Christmas, the one we dressed her in for her funeral.

"Fresno State is much harder than I imagined it would be before arriving there. I am only an average student compared to many of my classmates," I tried to explain.

"Average? You may be many things, but average is not one of them. I am sure there is not one other student who has had to work harder or who is doing more to put him or herself through college than you," she countered.

"I don't know of anyone who doesn't have someone supporting them. All the other students have family or, at least, a best friend. I have neither," I claimed.

"You always found a teacher to help you. Is there anybody at Fresno State?" she asked, pausing to give me time to respond.

"Well, I went to Fresno because of Coach Bochin. He's only eight years older than me, but he looks much older," I said, smiling and hoping to elicit a smile from Momma.

"Perhaps you can get him to help you," she suggested.

"The problem is that he spends a lot of time with students, but I don't think he is ready for someone like me, who cannot do the things he enjoys doing." I said. "He plays golf, and tennis, and bowls with them. He is a good chess player and he enjoys playing poker and other card games. But I cannot do any of these things. I feel totally left out," I admitted. "I just stand around and watch."

"But can't he help you with your forensics activities?" Mamma asked.

"Even with forensics I am not doing as well as I hoped to do. I have won a few trophies, but I have also failed to make the final round at a couple of tournaments," I admitted. "He tries to help all of us, but most of his time is spent with the debaters, who are very good. I am just beginning to learn how to debate."

"I have some suggestions for you. He is a teacher; tell him you have always wanted to learn how to play chess or to play poker or one of the other things you know he likes to do and ask him to teach you how to do it. But what have you done for him?"

"What do you mean? What could I do for him?"

"Have you ever offered to cut his hair as only you can do it? Have you ever offered to help him clean up his condo after a poker game? You should do things with him that will give him an opportunity to learn more about you. Do not think of him as a father figure; think of him as an older brother. Let him help you become the best speaker in the United States." she suggested; perhaps, demanded.

"I don't feel like I fit in with any of the professors. They are not like the teachers I had in high school, who saw me as a project," I declared.

"Perhaps college professors are there to guide you in your formal learning only. They direct you and give you options. You need to take the initiative to make the best out of each class and situation in which you find yourself. What else is bothering you?" she asked, and then was silent, waiting for my response.

"I am afraid I find myself enjoying alcohol too much. Almost everyone I have met drinks a lot and some smoke marijuana. Often I find myself doing things I don't ordinarily do if I am not drinking."

"I think drinking just makes it easier for you to do something you already want to do. Do not blame something or someone else for what you do. Liquor will never make you do something you don't want to do. You have often said that about your father."

"It allows me to do something I might consider doing but won't do on my own. I blame the alcohol instead of myself," I had to admit.

"If you want to do something, plan it out and evaluate the consequences, and do it; but own up to the choice you make. I think there is some other reason why you are here. Are you going to share it with me?" she asked.

"I don't think my life will ever matter. I wish I had died instead of you," I told her, looking down at the marker.

"You are my son. All my children are why I was placed on this earth. The world will be better because of each of you. You are already making a huge impact on all the other children in our family, your cousins, nephews, nieces, and friends, who will use you as a role model. You are just starting to live your life; don't think about death," she said, hoping to calm me.

"I have been thinking about me and my life. Every single person who comes to me to do their hair can find someone else almost as good as I, maybe even better. All the professors, especially, Dr. Bochin, have plenty of other students to mentor or make his protégées. When Father moved to Antioch, I had to leave my second family and several people I loved. I just don't see any real value in what I can offer anyone," I said. Before I could continue, Momma did what she always used to do, she reached out and pulled one of my hands toward her. She touched my face.

"Open your eyes and look directly into mine. I am your mother, and I am telling you that if you set your mind and soul on accomplishing something, you can do it. You have worked too hard to give up without a fight for your life. What do you think is the hardest and most worthwhile thing you can do now to show just how special you are?" she asked.

"Fresno State has never had a national persuasive speaking champion. Only one person in the entire U.S. can win that title each year," I told her.

"How do you stack up? When will this contest happen?" Momma asked.

"We are about two months away from the national tournament. Both Bob, another student who is great competitor, and I have qualified in two events. The chances of my winning are almost impossible," I confided.

"Did you hear what you just said? You said 'almost' impossible. Why can't it be you? Didn't you tell me that you went to Fresno State because you thought it fit your needs?" she asked, smiling that big smile she displayed when she knew she was giving me the ammunition to fight a good fight.

"I will have to re-write my persuasive speech," I clarified.

"What is it about?" she wanted to know.

"It is an evaluation of the Gay Liberation Movement and why we should accept people for what they are and not for what we want them to be," I explained.

"Your topic seems awfully persuasive to me. You can handle any editing that needs to be done. That is your specialty. What about what you should wear to this tournament. You always said that if you had better clothes, you thought you would do better. If that is true, do you have enough money to buy a new outfit?" she asked.

"The really good students, from the powerhouse schools, will be dressed in expensive and stylish suits," I told her.

"Maybe it is time for you to go clothes shopping. How many days do these contests last?" she asked, again waiting for my answer.

"Three days. You need to have three different outfits to maximize your speaking potential," I explained.

"So, you need three outfits. Do you have enough money?" Momma asked.

"I have some savings. I don't think I could ask anyone for help. There is a clothing store named "Patrick James," which Dr. Bochin has recommended to some of the debaters to get nice looking suits. They actually measure you and fit the suit to you!" I shared. "I suppose I could get something special to wear."

"Son let's get to the real reason why you are here. What are you thinking about doing to yourself?" Momma asked in the strongest voice she had yet uttered.

"I haven't made any specific decisions," I said. "I haven't totally given up. But if something happens to me, like a car accident on my drive back to Fresno; I don't think it would have much impact on most people and for some it might make their world better in the long run not to have me around," I confided.

"You think that all of the wonderful teachers and other people who have gone out of their way to prepare you to help others won't feel a loss for the energy, time, effort, and money they gave you to help you become a person capable of making wise decisions?" she questioned.

"I have tried to help. When I have an opportunity, I do try to help others. I am just one person," I said. I was still feeling sorry for myself and Momma noticed.

"Feeling sorry for yourself is not like you. Give love to all you meet. You may get hurt along the way but learn from everything you do and when you find yourself in a bad situation, make a change of direction that makes you and others better. I think you should get back in your car now and drive back to that college and make history," she said standing up so that I saw only a silhouette.

I refocused and realized that Momma was not there. There was no evidence she had ever been there, no chair, no marks on the grass of a rocker, no other person in the cemetery. I looked down at the name marker; the "Three Musketeers" wrapper was there, and it was half empty. I ate the rest of it.

When I got to my car, I noticed the half gallon bottle of vodka I had bought when I had gone into town earlier. I had thought about drinking enough vodka to give myself the courage to stop the loneliness and depression I had felt before my talk with Mamma. I wanted her to give me permission to take the easy way out of my situation. I planned to have a car accident occur as I drove back toward Fresno somewhere between Shafter and Delano. I wanted it to occur in the middle of the agricultural fields so everyone would know they had claimed another victim. I would get rid of the vodka bottle at the end of Laredo Highway as I entered the ramp onto Highway 99. No one could prove it was not an accident. It would look like I made a driving mistake changing lanes, swerved, and lost control.

My conversation with Momma had changed all that. Instead of approving of my plan, she had offered me hope and some new personal goals. I would start looking for women my own age to date. I would find things to do with Dr. Bochin and, hopefully, gain his personal and educational support. I would buy some suits I would be proud to wear at nationals. I would cut down my consumption of alcohol and stop blaming it for my bad decisions. Most importantly, I would edit and re-edit my persuasion speech until it was of championship caliber.

I opened the vodka bottle and instead of consuming it myself, I poured the contents on the road where I was parked beside Momma's grave. I would live to fight another day. I have gone back to the cemetery many times since that day. I talk with Momma and listen carefully to the advice she gives me. Of course, I thank her for always being there for me.

CHAPTER EIGHTEEN

After I returned to Fresno from visiting Momma's grave, I sat down immediately and wrote a "to do" list based on our recent conversation. Most importantly, I decided to follow Momma's advice and find a church full of like-minded worshipers who loved and understood the power of God.

At first, I thought it would be good for me to find a congregation that would allow me to slip in among the other followers, enjoy the singing, listen to the message, and leave without much investment. I decided to start with one of the mega-churches in the Fresno area. I discovered that attending it was much like going to a concert. There was a huge audience, a stage, a technical production team, cameras, lights, and action. It appeared to be staged, rehearsed, and slick. I felt nothing and talked to no one.

Next, I decided to try a smaller church. I drove around my neighborhood looking for a smaller-sized church building with local community involvement, much like the church I had attended in Wasco when I was healed some ten years earlier. I discovered First Church at the corner of Shields and Fruit Streets. A large sign told me there were three services per week: a Sunday morning, a Sunday evening, and a Wednesday evening service. The choir met Thursday evenings for rehearsal, and there was a Friday healing ministry. A temporary sign across the grassy area in front of the church informed people driving by about a special evangelist who would be conducting a service on the following Sunday. I liked what I saw from the outside, so I decided to visit the next Sunday morning to see what type of individuals attended this church.

As I entered the church building, I noticed several smiling faces, lined up on both sides of the lobby. Older persons, middle-aged adults, college aged men and women, and even younger children greeted those entering with smiles, handshakes, and hugs. The greeters appeared to gravitate toward those people entering who were similar in age to them. A young man, who appeared to be between twenty and twenty-five years old, noticed me and moved in my direction.

"Good morning. Welcome to First Church, where we accept you just as you are because God made you in his image and he loves you and so do we. My name is Nathan. Is this your first visit to our church?" he asked, smiling, and extending his hand for me to shake.

"Good morning. My name is Ron, and, yes, this is my first visit to your church," I responded, clasping his hand in mine.

"We are happy you decided to visit today. This will be a very special service. We have a guest speaker. I think you will find him an outstanding preacher," he said, handing me a service program.

"Great! I can't wait to hear him," I admitted. "I am a junior at Fresno State," I added, noting several people my age already seated in the church.

"We have quite a large youth and young adult group. There about thirty of us who also attend Fresno State, Fresno City, or Pacific College.

I would love to introduce you to some of the other college students after the service is over," he suggested, as he motioned for me to follow him.

"I would be happy to meet some people my age after the service," I told him and followed him into the main sanctuary. I noticed immediately what my former church called a "message board" in the front of the room. It showed the number of people who attended the last service (289), an outline of today's program, and the page numbers of the songs to be sung during the service. I sat down in the pew where Nathan directed me to sit. There were already many families, couples, and several college-aged people seated near me. As I sat down, I saw faces turning toward me and smiling and waving as though they knew me or were happy to see me.

If you save two spots next to you, my fiancée and I will come and sit with you once my duties at the front entry are completed," Nathan said. He walked back to the entry to the church. The church began to fill with people of all ages. I soon found the entire area near me, as well as the other pews, completely filled. There seemed to be no empty seats left. As the service was about to begin, the senior pastor came to the podium and made an announcement.

"Good morning, ladies and gentlemen. So many of our community members have come this morning to participate in our special service, we are going to be at full capacity. If you would help us by moving toward the center, so that people can fill in the rows from both sides, it will allow us to make sure everyone gets to be a part of what God has planned for us to share today," Pastor Givens instructed. The congregation moved almost in unison and soon everyone was seated. There was nothing exceptional about the beginning of the service. I recognized most of the hymns. The scriptures were also standard. I felt I was back at a service

I was used to. Then Pastor Given's introduced the visiting evangelist, "Ladies and gentlemen, Jerry Shaw," he said, moving away from the center of the stage and allowing the speaker to enter from the left side.

"Good morning, I am Jerry Shaw, and it is a privilege for me to be here today," he said. "I have only a limited amount of time, and God has much that needs to be done here today. Let me pray aloud. Heavenly Father bless your servant as I minister in your house of worship. Let those who have chosen to be here open their hearts and minds to your message. Allow them to step out in faith to receive that which you have for them today. Direct our attention to the things that will bring you honor and restore the faith to your servants waiting to hear your message. Amen."

He continued adapting his message to his audience: "God knows there are three distinct types of people here today needing His attention. First, there is a group who needs reassurance that God has not forsaken them, and He just needs you to talk to Him as you have done so many times before," voiced Pastor Shaw. "Next, there are some of you today who need healing. Some of you need physical healing and some of you need your heart, mind, and soul to be healed. You are loved and God wants you to become a voice of change in this world that needs people to be loved, accepted, and recognized as total human beings with all the rights that entails. You are to be a voice for those who are too scared and/ or unable to speak up for themselves," declared Pastor Jerry. "The third type of person here today wants to become more active within the church but does not know what talent he or she has that can be used. The church needs all kinds of talents. Each one of us sitting and standing before God today has talents this church can use to send the gospel message out into the community," confided Pastor Jerry. These words were getting close to my heart. I felt myself being revealed to him. I heard other members of the congregation call out that they were feeling the same way.

"Let us all stand and sing 'Amazing Grace.' God is healing, transforming, accepting, and changing lives right now. As we sing this song, raise your outstretched hands toward heaven and claim all that God has promised you. He will not disappoint," he promised, as the entire congregation began singing the familiar hymn.

I knew at that moment what I needed to do from this point forward, and that by doing as instructed, I would be able to help others. I decided in that moment that I was going to do my best to win a national title in persuasive speaking. If I could win first place, I would be worthy of consideration for any speech teaching job at any location where I might apply in the future. I would overcome all the odds that had faced me while growing up, in high school, and those encountered during my college years. God was going to allow me to become all I could be, so I could help others, and by helping others, I would help myself find who I really was born to be. I also knew that First Church was going to become my second home as long as I stayed in Fresno.

* * * * *

Second on my "to do" list was to fulfill my promise to Momma to get Dr. Bochin to be more of a mentor to me. I did not play the sports or card games that he enjoyed with other students, but there were other ways I could get closer to him. At my first opportunity to speak to him, I told him that Mike Weatherson had told me that he liked to play chess and that I wondered if he would teach me how to play. Much to my delight, he agreed; but I had some homework to do first. "Find a book about how to play chess and when you know the names of all the pieces, where they are placed on the board at the start of the game, and how each of them moves across the board, then come back and I will teach you how to play," Dr. Bochin promised. I immediately got a book from the library, learned what I needed to know, and returned a few days later to be tested. I passed.

Once we were playing, I casually mentioned that I was charging my clients $25 for a haircut. He was amazed, "Why that is five times as much as I pay," he said. "Are really charging that much?" he asked.

"Yes, but you have never had a professional like myself do your hair," I suggested. Would you like me to cut your hair sometime so you can experience the difference?" I asked him.

"Well, I am not ready to put out $25 for a haircut, but if you are willing to do it for a nice dinner at the restaurant of your choice, I would love to see what you can do," he offered.

"It will be my pleasure," I said, and we set a time and location. From playing chess, to cutting his hair, to going to movies, to helping him clean his condo after he had hosted a poker game; suddenly we could talk about anything. At last I had the mentor I had been looking for. Now I had to prepare for the national tournament.

I drove to the Patrick James clothing store with the intent of buying two suits and a sports coat which would make me one of the best dressed contestants at the national speech tournament in Chicago. As I opened the door and entered the main store, I was greeted by three employees. The suits, shirts, ties, and shoes were on display in various sections of the store. The display window had three mannequins, wearing complete suit outfits. One sported a traditional three-piece blue and black pinstriped suit, a coordinated shirt with colorful cufflinks, a pocket handkerchief, and a belt and shoes that matched. Another wore a denim two-piece suit with a blue shirt with cufflinks, a red, white, and blue tie, and again, matching shoes and belt in shiny black, giving it a definite splash of color.

One of the salespersons smiled as he moved toward me to shake my hand and welcome me to the store, "Welcome to Patrick James. My name is Oliver. Do you have an occasion to attend for which you want to look a step above everyone else?" he asked.

I shook his hand and returned his smile. "I will be representing Fresno State at the national speech finals in Chicago in ten days. I want to look as nice as, if not better than, all of the other competitors," I confided to Oliver.

"We have dressed many high school and college debaters before. We certainly can make your appearance a professional one that will meet our company's internal slogan of 'dress for more than success,'" he said, motioning for me to follow him to a section filled with traditional three-piece suits.

"I want it to be impeccable, but I don't want to have the same look as the traditional debaters," I explained.

"I see. You want to look like a photo shoot from the front cover of a contemporary fashionable men's magazine. I understand," Oliver responded.

"Please make me noticeable, but that notice must come from the color matching and fabric blending; a suit that says to everyone who sees it, 'My suit is not a JC Penney's special,'" I exclaimed.

"The newest color scheme is combining denim blue with expensive looking, thick, rich, buttoned collared shirts with accessories that will say this suit was made just for me by a top suit tailor. Our suit designer has been making suits fit people for over thirty years. He is the best in town. When you buy off the rack at a department store you take what you can get. We make your suit fit you right here! We measure you from top to bottom, your neck, your arms and legs, both internal and external seam lines. That, by itself, will make your tournament experience one of fashion and set you apart from all others," Oliver promised.

"Seems like I came to the right place," I agreed.

"With what kind of base price shall we begin our exploration?" he asked.

"I have five hundred dollars to spend," I replied. I had no idea how much suit that could buy.

"You are here at the perfect time. Today begins our buy two suits for the price of one sale. That means if you choose a suit at any price level, we can match another suit in that same price range for no additional cost," Oliver explained.

"So, I can buy one and get the other suit free?" I asked, making sure I had heard him correctly.

"Yes, as long as the other suit is not more expensive than the first," he clarified.

"Do I get a savings if the second suit costs less than the first?" I asked.

"No, cost is based on the higher priced suit. If you choose your second suit from those at the same price or lower, then that suit is free," Oliver stated.

"I see!" I stated. "That sounds good to me."

"In addition, you qualify for something else. Because you are a student at Fresno State, you may go to the front desk and pick from our free gift bowl a token that gives you a free accessory. You get one gift for each suit or jacket that you purchase. Shall we get started?" Oliver asked, already taking three suits from the rack that showed prices ranging from $400 to $500 a suit. Oliver took two suits over to a table that had shirts and ties already matched. He explained we would get the correct sizes later; but, at this stage we were only choosing color combinations. He wanted me to look at three different color combinations for each suit.

I liked a dark blue denim shirt, which had a slightly darker hue than the denim suit with a red, white, and blue tie, matching pocket hanky, and cufflinks that were a beautiful rich blue color.

"I can promise you not one other person will have this same suit at your tournament. Only five suits of this design have been created by our master tailor. We currently have four left. Pastor Hawkins from the Praise Church will be picking his suit up tomorrow," Oliver shared. I knew Hawkins was the senior pastor at the largest evangelical church in Fresno. They had three Sunday services with almost two thousand people attending each one. He was always impeccably dressed. If it was good enough for him, I was sure I would be dressed to the highest level. We spent the next thirty minutes having me try on the suit with all the accessories.

"You will be the best dressed man in Chicago," Oliver claimed as we finished with the first suit.

"I need the suit I will wear on the final day of competition to be a showstopper. My topic is slightly controversial, but all people hearing the speech will expect it to be offered by a man with high fashion sense, colorful, but, at the same time, tasteful," I shared, hoping to see just how colorful and tasteful Oliver could dress me.

"Our personal suit purveyor who buys many of our suits directly from the east coast manufacturing outlets returned yesterday. One of the suits be brought back from New York might be just what you need. We received only two of these suits. I started to make one of them up for our front window display a few minutes ago. Would you like to see it?" Oliver asked, motioning me to follow him to the back of the store through doors that had signs for employees only posted.

"Will this suit fit my budget?" I asked as we were approaching the doors.

"If you like it; I will make it fit," said Oliver, as he turned and gave me the following instructions. "Close your eyes. I will lead you and tell you when you can open your eyes... Now!" he instructed me.

As commanded, I opened my eyes. A blond and blue-eyed mannequin was positioned directly in front of me. He wore a bright red colored suit, trimmed with white colored seams, red and white buttons, and worn with a white shirt and a red and white tie. The cufflinks provided a red gem colored accent. A pocket handkerchief matched the tie and white leather shoes completed the outfit. Many people might think this color unacceptable and think it would not look elegant, but I fell in love with the suit immediately. It was stylish, colorful, yet very tasteful. I wore that suit for nationals and then in other formal settings. The suit certainly made this man. Comment cards from the national tournament judges complimented me and admired how the suit was so tasteful and bold. Several judges wrote that my suit made my topic and me more relevant and said that it helped make me more persuasive. I wish I had kept a picture of me in that suit for posterity. Unfortunately, I did not.

By the time I had finished, I had selected two suits and one sports jacket, a traditional blue blazer with gold buttons that I would wear at the tournament. I was now going to be Patrick James dressed for the tournament. I was given three chances in the drawings for accessories. None of the salespersons could believe my luck; I won three new pairs of shoes. I was told there were only three shoe picks in the bowl. Once the three salespersons found out that my goal to win nationals was why I had come to their store, they collectively pitched in to pay for the shirts, ties, and hankies. I only paid for the suits and the jacket.

As I was leaving the building with all my new accessories, I knew that God had once again moved people to help me so I could take my message forward in the most professionally dressed manner possible. I returned two days later to pick up the suits. Oliver told me to practice my speeches several times while wearing each of the suits so I would feel comfortable and make the suit an extension of me. I was glad I practiced in the new suits. The first few run-throughs found me paying attention to how I looked; yet after a few practices, the suits were simply part of my arsenal to persuade people willing to listen to my message.

* * * * *

A great week for me was about to get even better. Almost two years had passed since I had been asked to leave Aunt Alma and Uncle Skip's home because I would not renew my relationship with my biological father and would not agree to be on call to go to his house and help him with errands. My explaining to them why I would not see Father only caused us to drift further apart. They informed me that I had to put family first and would need to make Father a priority in my life. Since I could not do it, Aunt Alma asked me to leave.

About every six weeks I would make the three-hour trip from Fresno to Antioch to visit my sister, Sandy, either at her school or at the end of the school day, at a near-by fast food place. Sandy continued to live with them. Sandy and I had decided between the two of us to see one another even though Alma had forbidden us from communicating with each other.

I knew that over time they would learn my father's true personality and motivations. Eventually they would tire of his demands. When I returned home from Patrick James with my new suits, a letter was waiting for me. The letter was from Aunt Alma. I certainly did not know what to expect. I was afraid she might have learned about my visits with Sandy and her letter would be a formal cease and desist order. I opened the letter and began to read it:

"Dearest Ron, please read this letter completely before making any judgements. Let me, us, begin by apologizing to you for telling you that you had to love, respect, and help your father. We were trying to force a reconciliation and felt it would be good for all of us as a family. We did not think of the consequences of our demand. We have missed you every day. You brought to us a joy we had never experienced. We became your surrogate parents three days after you arrived in Antioch to work at Fiberboard. For those six months you lived with us, our family gained not only you, but your sister, Sandy, became our daughter. The two of you have made us whole."

"I take full responsibility for waiting so long to ask you to find it in your heart to forgive us. We need you to come back into our lives. We will never ask you or try to force you to do anything you are not comfortable with or don't want to do. As long as it does not harm you, we will protect you always."

"We want you to know that Uncle Bill is no longer here and will not be back. We should have listened to you. He used us as free transportation and as people to get him things. We gave him permission to use our credit card at the gas station and he not only got gas, but purchased tires, a tune-up, and had transmission work done on his car. That was before he gave it away to some woman. He bought groceries at the gas station without our knowledge or consent. We found out when Dallas, who owns the station, phoned, and asked when we wanted to catch up on our bill, which was then approaching $1,000. The grocery store called and wanted to know if we were authorizing Uncle Bill to continue shopping for liquor and cigarettes, as well as regular food. He had run up a tab of almost $2,000. The straw that broke the camel's back was when he told the hardware store owner, he could purchase anything in the store he wanted. He told him had us wrapped around his little finger and all he had to do was ask for something." I took a deep breath and continued reading the letter.

"Your father lived with five different women while he was here. I could tell you more, but this is enough to give you a feeling for what he has been doing. We gave him a one-way ticket back to Stigler, Oklahoma. We put him on the bus and told him he could not come back for our assistance and we let all the places in town know he was no longer able to use our credit. We waved good-bye to him and as soon as we got home, decided to ask you to forgive us. All of us want you back in our lives. We need you to be part of the family we were destined to be."

"We know we were wrong for letting you walk out of our lives. Please find it in your heart to give us another chance to be your surrogate parents. We will never let you down again. Call soon or write us back so we will know you will come home and be part of our family for the rest of our lives. Sandy, of course, misses you too. We told her what we are asking you to do and she thought we might have success if we wrote you and gave you some time to read and analyze our words." Mother continued, "It may take some time; but we are confident you will find it in your heart to allow us back into your life. We await your decision and forgiveness. Love, Mom and Dad."

I read the letter over five times that night. I had already forgiven them and was just waiting for the truth to set us all free to love each other as a family. I wrote a letter back to them that night. I mailed it to them the next day. My letter was short, "Dear Mom and Dad, forgive me for not staying and fighting for us. I will never leave you again. Your son, Ron."

CHAPTER NINETEEN

Bob and I flew to Chicago to represent Fresno State at the Tournament of Champions. As always Bob was impeccably dressed. He was tall, thin, and handsome. One could not meet him and not think he could be a clothes model. After hearing him speak, one might upgrade him to an actor or politician. In fact, he looked and sounded a lot like Omar Sharif.

Dr. Bochin selected Coach Dave Natharius to accompany us to the tournament because the woman Dave was dating was the coach at California State University, Los Angeles (CSULA), and she would be attending with a student who had qualified for the tournament. Dr. Natharius had made our plane, hotel, and tournament registration plans. We had not been told exactly where we would be staying in Chicago.

We took a shuttle from the airport to the hotel. I had done some research on my own to find the best hotels in which to stay when visiting Chicago. As we made our trip toward our hotel, we passed some of the places I had discovered, but we did not pull into any of them. Finally, the van let us out in front of an older building that looked tired and worn. The lobby had been nice once upon a time. Bob and I were staying in the same room. Coach N and the other coach were sharing a room; and the woman representing CSULA had her own room.

I felt this might be a once in a lifetime opportunity to visit Chicago and I wanted to find time to do some sight-seeing. Any location downtown would be near sight-seeing buses. When Bob and I walked into our room, we discovered that it was a step down from any room at Motel 6, where we had stayed in the past. There was a hole in the carpet with a throw rug over it that did not cover it completely. We opened the closet and there were no hangers on which to put our clothes. We both quickly arrived at the same conclusion. We did not want to stay in this hotel. We called Coach N and asked how much we were paying for our room. We could not believe it when he told us the excessive amount. I looked at Bob.

"This may be my only visit to Chicago, and I don't want this room to be a part of my memory," I said.

"It is not what I was expecting either. What do you think we should do?" asked Bob.

"Let's get out of here," I responded. I had an idea. We, two single and eligible men, were in Chicago to represent California and that is exactly what we should do. I called the Playboy Club to find out the price of their hotel rooms. It was fifty dollars per night higher than what we were paying for the "Squalid Inn." Bob and I decided to make a move. We called downstairs and complained to the front desk clerk about the condition of our room. We told him it was unacceptable. He informed us that there were no other rooms for us; they were completely booked up and had a waiting list. We told him we would be down quickly so they could have our room for someone on the waiting list. We also asked if the hotel would refund that day's room cost since they were going to re-rent our room. He told us our refund would be waiting. I called over and secured a room at the Playboy Club for us. Coach N said he would stay where he was and meet us each morning at the tournament.

The change from one hotel to another certainly can make a difference in how one feels about an experience. I had never been to any establishment that resembled this Playboy Club. We were both carded to make sure we were twenty-one. We both received a Playboy Bunny card that allowed us to enter the club where the famous bunnies served drinks. We went to our room. The Playboy Bunny emblem was on everything: the walls, bedspreads, towels, and even the toilet paper. After we got situated in our room, we decided to explore our new surroundings. We quickly noticed we were the two youngest males in the club. The experience we had there was one I will never forget. I will always remember the reaction we got from other students when we compared accommodations and they learned we were staying at the Playboy Club. Bob and I had the clothes, the style, and now the reputation of being what most people thought of as true Californians.

The next morning Coach N found me after my first round of the persuasive speaking competition. "How did your round go? Did you show them a new champion is in town?" he asked.

"That was the most competitive round I have ever encountered. All seven of us were perfect. If the rest of the rounds are like this one, I think we might be in for a long three days," I shared, after completing the best and most intense round of my life.

"Did you have any problems?" Coach N asked.

"No, I think I did as well as I could do!"

"Then I am sure you did fine!" he predicted.

I was relieved after my second round. When I saw Coach N after the second round, I did not want to brag, but I told him I was definitely the best. Round three was no different. I was confident I was the best. Two of my competitors asked me where I had purchased my denim suit. I looked great and the suit helped me speak even better because of the total confidence I now possessed.

The tournament staff announced the semi-final results for all the events in the auditorium where the final rounds would be performed. Both Bob and I had been participating in two events. We knew we could only advance in one event, but since we had not been contacted about this, we knew we had not made the cut in both events. Oral interpretation was announced first. Bob was named to the semi-finals. We were both very excited. I knew in my heart that his program was stronger than mine and that he deserved to be among the elite in this event. I was announced as a semi-finalist in persuasive speaking. The semi-final events took place at the same time in different rooms for all events.

I had been caught off guard when the semi-final round announcements were made for persuasive speaking. I was amazed. Of the fourteen speakers making it into the semi-final round, all seven from my first round had made it. I had to face three of them again in the semis, but I survived.

About an hour after the semi-final rounds ended. We found ourselves back in the auditorium waiting to see if either or both of us would advance to the finals. We both advanced.

The final round speakers performed in the large auditorium that had the plaques and trophies to be given to the finalists as a backdrop.

Bob shined as he performed his program during the final round of oral interpretation. I felt the worse placement he could earn would be third. If I were judging him and his program, he would have earned a first-place ranking from me.

I was the last contestant to speak in the persuasive finals. It was the best speech I have ever given. When I moved to the side the audience moved in that direction. At one point I just paused to take in the absolute feeling of speaking power that truth and people willing to listen can display. My red suit not only set me apart from the other speakers; it gave me additional confidence. I felt for the first time in my life that what I was doing and saying was the best I could ever do in any given moment. I felt I deserved to be the champion, but it was not up to me; I had to wait to see if the judges agreed. Bob placed fourth in oral interpretation. I placed first in persuasive speaking. Together, we captured second place in sweepstakes.

I was very fortunate. I was the right messenger at the right time, with the right topic, speaking to the right judges. I carried my first-place trophy onto the plane. It was too big to mail. The flight attendant allowed me to strap my trophy into an empty seat near mine. Once we were in the air, the captain made the following announcement: "Ladies and gentlemen, we are honored to be traveling with the college national champion in persuasive speaking today. You may have noticed the very large trophy beside him as you passed through the cabin. Congratulations are in order," he announced. At these words, the entire cabin began applauding. It was several weeks later that I learned that Bob had told the flight crew about my win, and they had informed the pilot. Bob has always been a man with great integrity and class.

As we flew home, I began reading the judges' comments. There was at least one comment each day about the suit I had chosen to wear, and they always noted how well tailored it was. I looked at the judge's rankings. There had been three judges in each round.

Round (1)	1st	1st	2nd
Round (2)	1st	1st	1st
Round (3)	1st	1st	1st
Semi-Finals	1st	1st	2nd
Finals	1st	1st	1st

I found one of the final round judge's comments to be the most rewarding: "When I noticed you were in the final round, I thought you might be at a disadvantage because I had judged you in round two of the competition and knew what you were going to say. You were even better in the final round!"

When we landed at the airport in Fresno, a group of students with signs and banners were there to greet us. Dr. Bochin was also present to tell us how impressed he was with both our performances. It was a trip I will never forget.

As early as the sixth grade, my goal in life was to graduate from college. I accomplished this just a few days after my twenty-third birthday, when I graduated from Fresno State with a major in speech communication and a minor in psychology. After moving from the Weathersons' home, I had spent my final two semesters living on my own. I had decided to do hair styling as often as possible and from that point on, I was financially able to meet my school and personal obligations. Aunt Alma, Uncle Skip, Sandy, and I had become a family again. I traveled back and forth to the Antioch area many times to celebrate holidays, birthdays, and anniversaries. Sometimes I helped by giving them a break from working seven days a week at the rest home they owned. They were in the audience for my graduation. My twin was not. After Donald had left them and gone into the armed forces, he had married and had three children by the time I graduated. We had not been communicating. I thought my new family was the family I had been meant to have because all of us needed each other. Later on, Skip and Alma would legally adopt Sandy and me, though we were already adults.

The Weathersons will always be the family that taught me how to share. I looked at the graduation audience and knew that I had made it through my junior college and Fresno State days because of the help of people like them, whom God had placed in my life to love and support me when I most needed it. We don't do things on our own. We accomplish things with the help of others. We are the result of all who cross our paths. I was very proud I graduated *magna cum laude* because I transferred all the horrible grades from my second semester at Bethany. Had I known then what I know now, I would have just started college without claiming them.

Even though I had graduated with honors, the most rewarding part about earning my Bachelor of Arts degree was that I had fulfilled my commitment to Momma. She would have been so proud of me. I was proud enough for both of us. When things got difficult and I had little drive or will to continue, I recalled the conversations we had shared, and I found the strength to overcome all the obstacles that were thrown in my direction.

* * * * *

I decided to remain at Fresno State for my Master of Arts degree. I was heavily recruited by CSU, Long Beach, to assist with their forensics program, but I still didn't feel I would be able to adjust to living in the Los Angeles area. It was all I could do to visit there during tournaments. I decided it would be too stressful to live with the chaos of traffic, housing, people, and living styles that I was unprepared to meet.

I wanted to complete a typical two-year M.A. program in one year. I had to seek permission from the dean of the graduate school at Fresno. I met with him and explained that I was putting myself through college and had been carrying over twenty units each semester as an undergraduate at Fresno State.

The dean finally approved my petition to complete my M.A. program in a one-year time period. The Speech Department had never allowed any student to attempt the program any differently from the way outlined in the M.A. program guidelines, which assumed a two-year time frame; but they made an exception for me.

A few of the speech professors had recently finished their own degrees or were in the final stages of completing their Ph.D. programs. Some of them thought it best for others to follow the same path that had been required of them. They felt a M.A. degree needed two to three years to complete and a Ph.D. program at least three or four years. To this day, I know of only two people anywhere who completed their M.A.'s in a single year.

To complete my program, I had to find three faculty to become members of my MA committee. Two of them had to be within the speech department and one from outside the department. They had to be familiar with me as a student and be willing to examine my performance in written exams.

At first, I wanted to ask Dr. Bochin to serve as my committee chair, but outside of forensics, I had taken only one class from him and that was not even an upper division one. I did not want to have to study the materials he would normally test a student on since I was not familiar with them.

I had taken some upper division classes from Dr. George Diestel, who was known to be a very demanding professor, smart, but fair. I was familiar with the type of questions he might ask, and I had done well in his classes. He was not bothered by my trying to finish my degree quickly and he readily agreed to chair my committee. He spent quite a few hours during that year helping me become a much better researcher and writer.

Dr. David Natharius had taught two speech classes I found to be very interesting: theories of group discussion and interpersonal communication. He too thought I could take a large number of classes each semester and get prepared for exams at the same time. He became my second inside member.

The outside committee member was the easiest choice for me. I asked Dr. Holder, the chair of the psychology department, if he would serve on my committee. I had taken an upper division course from him. I had minored in psychology and felt such classes gave me a definite advantage in understanding how and why people use communication to express themselves and to influence others.

I was pleased that each of these busy faculty members agreed to mentor me by serving on my committee. Dr. Natharius was going to head our forensics team during the year of my forensics assistantship. I felt his constant oversight of my ability to coach, to make reservations, to complete tournament entry forms, to travel with students, to evaluate students from other colleges, and to help our own students with their preparation would be an advantage to me since I wanted to coach at the college level.

* * * * *

I continued to style hair, was a graduate assistant in the forensics program, and was carrying one year's worth of classes each semester. Dr. Natharius inherited a fixer-upper home just before the fall semester started. He told me I could rent a room from him. He warned me that people would be coming and going, day and night, to help with the renovation. These people showed up to fix floors, cabinets, walls, sinks, ceilings, windows, and transform the yard. He already had Dr. Diestel occupying the second of his three bedrooms. Both professors were divorced and between partners. Both thought they could help me stay on task if I lived in the same household. Both were willing and able to provide additional academic reports I should examine, suggest guest speakers for me to find time to meet, greet, and talk with when possible; they also provided additional reading on subjects they felt important, whether I asked for them or not. I must say, they both worked hard, and they partied just as hard. They had recently finished their terminal degrees and I quickly found our house was a mecca for many social gatherings.

I started spending more time at the library studying because many evenings our home was filled with people. At the same time, I was fortunate that they were willing to share and to teach me things about life I had never experienced before. It was the first time I met someone who was changing gender, openly gay women and men, hard drinkers, and pot smokers. Earlier in my life, I had thought these kinds of people were sinners and degenerates. I discovered that they are people too. I loved the fact that both of my mentors were willing to accept anyone entering our home at face value. If any person got too drunk, became obnoxious, or was trespassing on any other person's self or ideas, they were quick to reprimand them or ask them to leave.

During the second semester of my graduate work, I pushed myself to my limits. When my mother had been in the hospital dying, I had learned to go on very limited sleep, but this time I was expected to function academically at a high level when all I wanted to do was get some rest.

When finals week arrived, I was taking twenty-one units of classes and dealing with seven in-class finals; I was also taking the comprehensive exams for my degree in lieu of writing a M.A. thesis. I had gone three days without any sleep. All I was doing was studying for finals and the three to four-hour exams in four areas of my communication emphasis.

Around 4:00 a.m. one morning, I found myself falling asleep and felt I needed something to help me stay awake, so I made some coffee. I had never drunk coffee before. I didn't even like the smell of it. Because I had not been eating properly and had gone so long without sleep, the coffee upset my stomach and I began throwing up. I blamed the coffee though, of course, it was my fault. Even today, however, I refuse to drink coffee.

Not only was I taking exams but was also interviewing at several colleges to become their forensics coach. I eventually accepted the Bakersfield College position because it allowed me to return to the agricultural area where I had been raised. I wanted to be a role model for others who wanted to leave the fields.

I don't have any memory of that final week after I got sick from the coffee. I was told that I defended well both my written answers and the ad hoc questions asked by other faculty members who could question me. I had been given the opportunity to elaborate, to present new data that was not discussed in my written answers, and to clarify any details that may have been left out or not addressed in my written answers. I was also told that one faculty member was especially hard on me during his questioning time and, apparently, did not want the committee to award me a degree. I don't remember that person even being at the exams or my oral defense. I have tried to remember that week and the details of what took place. I have no personal memory of what happened. A few trusted faculty members since that time have shared what they remembered with me. I have no reason to doubt what I have been told.

What I do remember clearly is that at the conclusion of my defense, the committee retired to deliberate. Dr. Diestel had informed me they would leave the room and let the candidate reflect on the answers he had provided. He shared with me that this waiting game was part of academic tradition. I had learned of a couple prior students who had not been awarded their degree until they had retaken certain course content and been retested by their committees. While my committee was out deliberating, I am sure that thoughts of failure crossed my mind; however, I did not expect such an outcome. Dr. Diestel, my chair, had also shared with me the importance of the written questions and how it was up to me to substantiate any areas of concern or additional development requested by committee or by other faculty members during the defense stage. I am sure I tried to be as clear as possible and to explain any weaknesses that may have appeared in my written answers. When the committee finally returned, none were smiling.

Dr. Diestel walked over to me and I stood. He placed one hand on my shoulder and shook my hand with a smile and hug. I had passed! For any faculty who were not supportive of the decision to grant me my M.A., I hope my accomplishments since earning my M.A. have made them feel better about my committee voting to award me a degree. I have tried to give back to the schools, where I have been blessed to teach, by mentoring and motivating other students like myself who were not traditionally seen as college material, but who now are doctors, lawyers, judges, congress people, business owners, teachers, college professors, and even famous television producers, series creators, and professional actors. I know I have had a positive influence in allowing them to find their self-worth.

By the time I turned twenty-four, I had earned my M.A. I had completed my B.A. and M.A. in a total of five years. Throughout my long teaching career, what I learned from Dr. Bochin, Dr. Diestel, Dr. Natharius, and Dr. Holder has stayed with me. They taught me respect for students, the importance of making academics challenging, the role of a facilitator, and the willingness to accept people on their own level and to allow them to progress to the limits they chose.

My college years were instrumental in developing me as a teacher, a coach, and as being the person of whom, someday when I die, others might say, "He did so much with so little." All the good I have done and shared is because of what others were willing to share and teach me. Any mistakes I made were my own.

CHAPTER TWENTY

When I interviewed at Bakersfield College for the Director of Forensics position, one of the other candidates told me that the local high schools were always looking for teachers in the areas of speech and English. As I drove back to Fresno, I decided to do some research to find out if teaching at the high school level in an area like Bakersfield would qualify me for the forgiveness feature of my loan and I could have some of my student loan debt reduced by teaching there. I found out that it did.

Since I would not be hearing from the college for a while, I decided to try to earn a secondary teaching credential within the next six weeks. I learned I had to earn twenty-seven units in the short time I had. I met with the Fresno State credentialing specialist. She explained there was a limit of twelve units one could take during summer school. She also informed me I was too late to be admitted to that summer's student teaching cadre. The twenty-seven units were far too many units to accomplish in a summer session at Fresno State.

I asked if I were to attend other colleges and transferred those other units by the end of summer if those college units would be acceptable and be allowed to apply toward my credential. She did not like the idea because she felt it was a dangerous precedent to set; but in the end, she agreed that nothing would or could prevent it. I then asked if any community college coursework could be transferred or used toward the college credential program. After consulting with her supervisor and looking at the relevant education codes, she told me that a maximum of three units from a community college, used as an elective in the general area of English grammar, would be acceptable, toward the credential, if it had not been used to meet any undergraduate requirement.

I went to Fresno Pacific College, a private Christian university, and met with Dr. Murphy, their secondary teaching specialist. He informed me that one of his student teachers, who was supposed to begin student teaching the next morning, had found a very well-paying job for the summer and notified him that he would postpone his student teaching to the fall instead of doing it that summer. He was scheduled to teach at Edison High School from 8:30 a.m. until 12:00 p.m., five days a week. Dr. Murphy told me he had an opening in his 6:00 a.m. to 8:00 a.m. course on how to write behavioral objectives. By the end of the day, I was enrolled in some type of class Monday through Thursday from 6:00 a.m. until 10:00 p.m. I planned to keep my Saturday and Sunday hair styling appointments since I could see at least twenty clients each day.

The regular credentialing courses at Fresno State were typical lecture classes, with book readings, some discussion, some presentations, papers, and two had a project. Those three classes accounted for nine units. One course at Fresno City was three units, and student teaching sponsored by Pacific College, which was the most challenging for many reasons, accounted for twelve units. Dr. Murphy's morning course offered three additional units. I decided to transfer all the units I was taking to Fresno Pacific College instead of to Fresno State.

* * * * *

Dr. Murphy went with me to meet the supervising teacher who would be my mentor and role model. His name was Stephen Mandelin. Dr. Murphy told me Steve was one of his favorite master supervising teachers because he shared his own lesson plans as examples to student teachers, watched their presentations without interrupting or interfering unless absolutely necessary, and answered questions as they arose each day. Mandelin had developed a special handout for his perspective teachers on high school discipline, in which he identified what should be done and what should never be done.

Mandelin was teaching basic grammar to seniors needing the class to complete their high school graduation requirement and who had failed it at least twice before. I called this class "The SVO Class." Subject, verb, and object are the three parts of speech that need to be understood to know how to write. I thought this class would be something I would enjoy teaching very much.

We arrived thirty minutes before the class at Edison was to begin. I explained I had just completed my Master of Arts degree but thought I might benefit by having a teaching credential that would allow me to teach from the sixth grade through high school. Mandelin suggested I sit in the back for the first day and observe his interactions with the class. He shared with me that he would introduce me as a fellow teacher, who would be making a student's journey in summer school more enjoyable and that we were both equally qualified to teach the class and were team-teaching it.

Dr. Murphy left us, and we started discussing what was planned for the first day. Mr. Mandelin, who told me to call him Steve when not in class, let me know he was also the assistant vice-principal in charge of discipline. He warned me that he might be called out of class from time to time to handle a disciplinary problem. He liked having student teachers because they could immediately take over his class and the students would never be without a teacher in the room.

The class started and I was introduced as Mr. Reel by Mr. Mandelin, who explained that we were team teaching the class. One of the students, who was over six feet tall and looked to be my age, raised his hand.

"I heard that when you team teach with these people, they aren't real teachers," he said, smiling and getting a high-five from the person sitting across from him.

"I don't know what you heard or thought you heard; but rest assured Mr. Reel or any other teacher who is teaching with me in this classroom is fully qualified, state approved, and most importantly, for whatever reason, he has chosen to be here, he is here to help you knuckleheads. Don't challenge Mr. Reel, me, or the system. Sit back and let's get ready to learn. As with any great team-teaching duo, only one of us can teach at a time. I am up first, and Mr. Reel will be sitting at the back of the class taking notes on how each of you are participating, paying attention, and trying to understand the material we are covering," he explained to the class.

I walked to the back of the room and took my seat at a duplicate of the desk at the front of the class. I quickly found out I was watching a master teacher at work. Steve told the class we were going to break down sentence structure to the barest element which could be equated to prehistoric development of language from the time men and women just grunted and began the evolutionary cycle. He indicated that by the end of summer school those students who paid attention could form sentences that could be several lines long. He told them that what they would learn to do would be a far cry from just two-word sentences.

"Writing or speaking English is using words to describe what is taking place. Today we are going to learn three parts of that process. I have written the first two parts on the board. In your textbook they are called subject and verb. We are going to make this so easy that some of you will leave class today and go home and be able to impress your parents so much they will think you should leave home immediately and enroll in college. First, we need to define and understand what is a subject and then what is a verb. Remember, basics first and advanced information after we understand the basics. Today's subject will be proper nouns. We will use people's names. Verbs will be actions. Our subject on the blackboard is which word? Let me give you a hint, it is a person's name. Raise your hand if you know?" he asked. Almost every hand went up. Just at that moment, however, someone opened the door and interrupted the class.

"Mr. Mandelin, I am sorry to bother you, but you are needed in the office. It is an emergency," said a woman in her late forties or early fifties.

"I will be right there," he said as he motioned for me to come to the front of the room. As I approached the front, I heard him say:

"I need Mr. Reel to take over and you need to remember he is acting for me and you are too do whatever he asks of you. I will be back as soon as I can," he said, leaving the classroom in my hands.

Looking out at the class from the front of the room and seeing their faces instead of the backs of their heads was much more frightening.

About half of the boys could pass for college seniors and about the same percentage of the girls would never be carded in a bar.

"Let's start where Mr. Mandelin left off," I said walking to the backboard to take a piece of chalk so I could write when needed. There was a voice coming from the back; I could not see who was talking.

"So, Mr. Reel, you some sweet rich white boy commin in here to save us by learning us how to write good even if we don't plan on writtin much in our life cause we want our talkin to be our callin card?" he asked. I thought for just a minute about how to handle this situation. We had not addressed this situation in any of the "how to teach" classes, nor had this kind of confrontation been addressed with Steve.

"We need to make some ground rules so all of us know what is expected. If you want to ask a question, you must raise your hand and be recognized. We will have no more shouting or uncontrolled chaos. I will begin modeling acceptable behavior by asking whoever asked me the last question to identify himself. I will answer your question this time. From now on, however, you must be recognized before asking a question and your question must be about the subject under discussion. Now, who asked the question," I asked. I looked up and down the rows. Slightly off center to the right in the last chair of that row I saw a hand waving.

"Thank you for participating. We are learning together to be respectful of each other. What is your name?" I asked him, not knowing if I would get an answer or what would happen.

"Jeramiah, Jeramiah Jenson," the student said.

"Jeramiah let me address your question, which had several parts to it. The question you constructed is in fact a complex, compound, run-on sentence. By the end of the semester we will use it to measure how much progress we will have made concerning how to make it a legitimate sentence with action, description, and texture. First, I am not a rich white boy. My parents were farm laborers who could neither read nor write; and who, with the help of my brothers and sisters, picked cotton, potatoes, grapes, and other vegetables and fruits in the central valley between here and Bakersfield. My mother was a Cherokee Indian, and my Father is Irish. I have nine brothers and sisters and only four of us are light skinned. Second, I have not come here to "learn" you anything. I am here to teach you how to express yourselves better. We will not learn to write good; but instead, we will become good writers who write well. Third, the amount of writing you do in your lifetime will be entirely up to you. What I want to happen is that your writing, not 'writin', will be deliberate and help you say exactly what you mean. Fourth, you should know that you lucked out by having me as your teacher. A few years ago, I was the first student in the history of Fresno State to win first place in persuasive speaking at the national finals level. I was born and raised under the same conditions as most of you. If I can overcome poverty, go to college, and graduate, so can you," I concluded. The classroom was quiet. One of the girls started applauding, she was joined by another student, then another; soon the entire class was applauding, smiling, and being respectful. One of their own had made it and they felt their plight was not as fatal as they had imagined it before today.

"Now, back to our lesson. What is the subject's name?" I asked.

"John" said the class in unison. I started walking toward the various rows and pointing at various students.

What is your name? What is your name? What is your name?" I asked about ten students.

"A person's name is a proper noun. Take a sheet of paper out and place it on your desk. Take a pen or pencil and write the noun that is on the blackboard. Look at the second word. That word describes the action John is doing. What is John doing?" I asked. Almost everyone said he was running.

"The words on the blackboard are only two; it says, 'John ran.' This is so simple. That's why it is called a simple sentence. It can be identified as a subject and verb constructed sentence. We call it an SV sentence. It is very simple to remember: the name of a person plus the action he or she does. Class let's look at some other types of sentences that will show how to construct a simple sentence," I said walking to the blackboard. I wrote the following words: "Jan sits. April sings. Keith laughs."

"When I point to you, tell me your answer. Use your own name as the subject and then tell us an action you like to do," I instructed them. I started pointing. They responded quickly.

"Penny reads. Ty cooks. Sarah swims. Fred farts." When the class heard Fred's answer many started to laugh. We were all laughing together when Mr. Mandelin returned to class. I shared with him that the class understood S-V sentences and were now ready to learn the "O" or the object part of the lesson.

I can say in all modesty that I hit a home run with the class that day. As I look back on it, I know it could have gone in many different ways. When you are teaching or facilitating discussions, I learned that you must be authentic, caring, and helpful. Those six weeks of learning how to become a credentialed teacher made me a better teacher at every level. Many professors, as they begin their careers, have never taught before and know very little about lesson plans. They may never have thought about different teaching strategies. By the end of summer school, I was exhausted. I had worked harder than I ever imagined possible, but I knew that in the end, I was a better person and a better teacher than I was before the summer started. I was now a credentialed teacher and the state of California would allow me to teach in any grade between sixth and twelfth should I so desire. As it turned out, however, I accepted the job in Bakersfield and began my teaching career at Bakersfield Junior College.

CHAPTER TWENTY-ONE

As I turned the key in the ignition to start the U-Haul truck, which contained all my possessions and was towing my car, I felt very happy. I had dreamed of this moment for years. Not only had I graduated from college, but I had earned an M.A. degree and was about to start teaching full-time at Bakersfield Junior College. As I drove south on CA 99, I thought it would be a good time for me to count the many blessings I had received during my college years.

The Waldrip family was responsible for my being able to take the first major step forward toward receiving a college degree. I am sure their insisting I travel with Marilyn, their daughter, from Wasco to Santa Cruz was just an excuse to make sure I had a way of getting safely to Bethany. They even provided me with a package of things I would need to set up a dorm room, essentials I had not even thought of.

Barbara, the administrative secretary at Bethany, was not just a random person working in an office on the one day I needed her most; God had placed her there. She took the initiative to question and support me when Mrs. Hensley had scored my entry exam using the wrong answer sheet. She believed me when I insisted that I had passed the test and she sought out a path to prove that what I said was true. Her intervention allowed me to be placed in tougher classes, where I met other students whom I needed to meet, and who also needed something from me.

Of all the roommates I could have been assigned, I was blessed with Rich, who not only shared his clothes and his allowance with me; but best of all, his parents, who did not know me, helped me purchase a car when I needed one. They followed God's direction and stepped out in faith, knowing I would live up to the faith they had in me by repaying them for their generosity. (Their kind deed came full circle when, many years later, and long after his parents had died, I was able to help Rich, when he was very ill and needed financial assistance).

One of the greatest blessings bestowed upon me took place when my brother Joe helped me get the job at Fiberboard during the summer of 1969. Aunt Alma and Uncle Skip were sent by God to welcome me the second night I arrived for my summer job. God knew I needed parents and they needed a son. As I embraced my new family, a new obstacle was placed before me. My new mom became very ill. Taking my new family's advice, I left Bethany and enrolled at San Joaquin Delta College so I could be close by and help care for her. We became a family. They never once tried to replace Momma, but over the years I learned to love them just as much as I had loved my biological parent. They eventually adopted me and my sister Sandy.

Speech coach Ginger Vogler at San Joaquin Delta College took me under her wings and taught me about forensics. She is responsible for my learning how to do research, to edit my own work, and to rehearse what I want to say. I was responsible for her learning that hairstyling can be done correctly by the person you least expect in a time of turmoil. When another Delta professor challenged my integrity, Ginger came to my aid and forced that person, who did not believe anyone who came from an agricultural background could write well, and therefore had accused me of plagiarism, to back down and to accept my work as my own.

The day I left the home of my aunt and uncle because I would not become the one to fetch items for my biological father, a perfect stranger helped me. God sent someone to offer to drive me across the river levees between Antioch and Stockton and made sure I was protected while I was experiencing one of my lowest bouts of rejection.

Mrs. Hanson knew exactly what she needed to return her salon to the high level she had become accustomed to during its prime time. She was sure of herself and was not willing to leave anything to chance. Her calculations paid off for both of us. She was careful to make not only me, but all the other stylists live up to their potential. Had I not charged the high prices she demanded, I would have been forced to work much longer hours and my studies and education certainly would have suffered.

Dr. Bochin's influence was the most subtle and long lasting. God knew I needed someone to emulate so He placed me under the direction of a person who could help me find the best in me; and by doing so, I was able to find the same quality in others during my own teaching career. His assistance with a textbook scholarship was the icing on the cake and allowed me the opportunity to purchase the many texts I needed for the high number of classes I undertook every semester. Dr. Bochin has always looked after my interests.

The job at Tinkler Mission Chapel was sent directly from God because it came at the exact moment, I needed it, so I could learn to be independent and not to rely on others. Not many people can work in a mortuary, let alone in a facility that did not value or support the well-being of its employees. I feel that God sent me there to confront the constant abusive behavior and lack of respect for the law that was condoned by the administrators. My protest went unheard, but at least someone was speaking out for better treatment of the dead.

The Weatherson family taught me about love, respect, and acceptance. Family members had differences and issues; but what they possessed the most was respect and acceptance of each other. Differences never resulted in screaming at each other, demeaning each other, and most importantly, they never physically abused each other. Love is all about support, encouragement, and establishing obtainable goals. Contrary to popular belief, sometimes love does mean having to say, "I am sorry."

I was given a great gift by the Patrick James employees in my quest to win the national tournament. I often asked myself what would have happened if these specific people had not been working in the store that day I shopped there. Each one of them decided to contribute some of his own money to help me clothe myself to the level that made my wardrobe just a bit superior to that worn by all other contestants at nationals.

Our graduate assistant, Susan, spent countless hours helping me to rewrite, stage, and prepare every word in my speech so that the message would be as clear and as persuasive as humanly possible. If I had come to Fresno a year earlier or a year later, I would not have received the benefit of her help.

God saw to it that Dr. Diestel, Dr. Natharius, and Dr. Holder, all very busy men, agreed to become members of my M.A. committee and did everything in their power to prepare me for completing my terminal degree at Fresno State. I learned much from each of them independently and from the three of them collectively. I will be forever grateful for their willingness to give me a chance to overcome what some had thought an insurmountable obstacle in record time.

Dr. Murphy at Fresno Pacific College became my advisor and mentor for my secondary teaching credential. It was not a random act that one of his student teachers, who was supposed to begin student teaching the day after we met, gave notice only a few minutes before I talked with Dr. Murphy and he told me this student was not going to student teach that summer. Miraculously, the college needed a student teacher and I just happened to be available. God does help those willing to work and help themselves.

It was also not coincidental that of all the student teachers assigned to Fresno Pacific College, I was given the opportunity to be taught and mentored by Mr. Mandelin, who was correctly identified as a master teacher. His tutelage prepared me to handle every situation that arose during my junior and senior high teaching days.

One of my regrets from my college years in Fresno is the fact that I did not spend as much time with Pastor Givens from First Church as I would have liked. Between preparing for nationals, completing my M.A. in nine months, and earning my secondary teaching credential in six weeks, I had very little time to devote to ongoing church services. I will always cherish the acceptance and the love that was given to me by a church that accepts people at face value because God creates all of us, and that makes all of us right.

The list of the blessings I had received could have been longer but in a very short time I was driving by the Shafter exit of CA 99 and passing Laredo Highway, when I thought about Momma, buried a few miles away. My mother was the most important of God's gifts to me. Even in death she gave my life direction. During my college years I felt I needed to go to the cemetery to be close to her and to be loved by her. As the years passed, I realized I could talk to her from any place and on any occasion. Her answers were always clear, and she was quick to point out that by taking the high road, never compromising your integrity, and supporting others, we leave the world a better place than it was when we entered it. Momma was always ready to talk whenever a problem bothered me.

Now I noticed I was fast approaching the Oildale exit that would take me past the college and eventually to my new home. Panorama Drive, home of Buck Owens, would lead me past the college. As I started the curve going up to the larger homes, I noticed two houses that were much smaller. Mary Copelin, my beloved forensics coach at Bakersfield, lived in one of them. She was responsible for teaching me the true art of rewriting the content of a speech. I learned from her that the more one researches and collects current information about a topic, the better one can discuss that topic.

Just past Bakersfield College, I turned right and was soon on Christmas Tree Lane. How appropriate that my favorite time of the year and my love for decorating for that holiday would become the street name of the first residence I would have after graduation. I had secured an apartment two blocks from the college. I learned that four other college professors lived in the same building. There were two PE instructors, who were also weightlifters, a music instructor, and an English professor. The apartments were larger than most in size and they came with a garage. It was hot in Bakersfield during the summers and cold during the winters. A garage would be appreciated when returning late at night or during the rainy season. When I got to the apartment building, the weightlifters were outside relaxing on the front stoop. They quickly volunteered to help me move my furniture from the U-Haul. It took us about thirty minutes to place all my possessions into my unit. I offered to take them to dinner but was told that they had a very special eating regime, which they did not want to change. Instead, I gave them fifty dollars and told them that they could use this to buy the items they needed for their special diet.

*   *   *   *   *

My department chair had explained to me that to complete my teaching load, I would have to teach two evening classes in different towns on two separate nights. I was scheduled to teach beginning public speaking in Wasco and in Tehachapi. Wasco, my birthplace, was north of Bakersfield about twenty-six miles and Tehachapi was east of Bakersfield about the same distance. She also informed me that the average age of the students taking these classes was about fifty-five years old. This information caused me to use my imagination to create an opening night experience for them so they would accept me as their instructor even though I was less than half their age.

I arrived at Tehachapi about an hour before my class was to begin. I set my handouts, book, and syllabi on the desk that was closest to the entry door. I sat in the last seat in the row furthest from the entry and waited for the students to arrive. As the students began to come in, I introduced myself to them individually.

"Hi, my name is Ron. What's your name?" I asked the first student to arrive. The gentleman looked the age of my father, who was then sixty-two.

"My name is Randall. I must do a bunch of talking to other managers, so I decided I would try this class out and see if it can help me. You are smart to learn how to talk at your age. You look about the same age as my son," he told me. I wanted to stop him before he asked me if I knew his son or why I was taking this class at night.

"I hope this class teaches us all to be better communicators," I declared as two more students arrived. I quickly welcomed them.

The class was scheduled to begin at 7:00 p.m. "Where the hell do you think the instructor for this class might be?" asked one of the older gentlemen at a few minutes past the hour.

"If they have never been to Tehachapi or to this high school before, they might have miscalculated how much time it takes to get here," responded one of the women.

The class became slightly agitated when it became 7:15 p.m. and the instructor still had not made an appearance. I decided it was time for me to take charge.

"Since we are all here and class should have started, why don't we introduce ourselves and tell why we are taking this class so that we will know each other better," I suggested. I asked the woman seated in the first seat of row one to introduce herself. She rose to the occasion and stood and shared with us her name and what she was expecting to get out of the class. One by one, the students dutifully stood up and shared their names, why they were taking the class, and what they were hoping to learn. A few shared their age. It was finally my turn. I stood and began walking toward the front of the class.

"My name is Ron Reel and I am the professor assigned to teach this class," I said, looking around the room. Suddenly the class became very quiet. The carefree class had disappeared. The students were sitting upright, and some were truly confused that someone my age was their instructor.

"Remember how all of you were smiling, sharing, and not so tense before you knew the teacher was here. I want an atmosphere of acceptance, respect, and as little stress as possible during our class. Each of you can succeed if you depend on yourself and on me. I will not let you make a fool of yourself. I am the only national champion public speaker in Fresno State's history. I completed my master's degree in one year. Some may think I am smart. I say I am dedicated and work harder than most. I will provide you with all the tools you need to succeed. I have worked in the agricultural fields in McFarland, Delano, Wasco, Shafter, and Arvin. My parents could not read nor write. Teachers made a difference in my life. I want to be that teacher for you. As a class, we will want each other to do the best job possible. You will be safe, and you do not need to be afraid. I will make this promise to you: this will be a respectful classroom for you to learn how to speak before others. All you must do is stay enrolled in our class and try. I won't let you fail if you complete all of your assignments," I said, smiling and waiting for them to respond. One by one they started clapping and within a couple of seconds, the entire class was standing and applauding.

The applause was not for me. It was for the environment and the commitment that had been made by all of us to respect each other and to provide a classroom that was a learning environment for what many consider to be the most frightful experience a human can have, making a public presentation.

I felt good about the outcome of week one in the Tehachapi class. Week two was even more meaningful to me. One of the older female students lingered after class was dismissed. She walked toward me carrying some papers in her hand.

"After class last week, I went home and dug through some of my old tax information. My husband and I were farmers in the McFarland-Delano area. I thought you might want to see these old paystubs that have your parents' names on them. This one is even more significant. Your name is on this paystub. You have come so far, and I am honored to be learning under your tutelage," she said, smiling and handing the papers to me. "You made it. Help others do the same. We can't do it alone. We all need help."

I spent the next forty years of my life in education. After two years at Bakersfield Junior College, I became the director of forensics at Bakersfield High School, where I sent students to the state and national finals, giving them the same experiences I had received. I continued to travel back to Fresno on weekends while I handled twenty to twenty-five hair appointments to supplement my income. I left Bakersfield in 1979 and moved back to Antioch. During the year I reflected on what was truly important to me as I made plans to go forward.

POSTSCRIPT

In 1980 I moved back to Fresno, accepting a teaching and forensics coaching position at New Life Christian High School. I assembled an incredible group of forensics students who far exceeded my expectations in terms of awards won and willingness to work. Unfortunately, the senior pastor of the church and school made a million-dollar investing "mistake" and the school closed without notice and without paying the faculty their final monthly check.

I accepted a job in Clovis, California, at a well-respected high school in the Fresno suburban area. I found to my delight that Pastor Earl Gould, the minister from Wasco, who had supported me during my high school years, had accepted a job as student counselor there. After an exciting year and half in Clovis, I spent a few years in school administration, starting as a vice principal in Covina, California.

In 1987 Mt. San Antonio College, the largest single campus community college in California, advertised for a speech position that included starting a forensics program. Tired of school administration, I applied for and got what turned out to be my dream job. During the next twenty-five years, I would not only direct one of the most successful forensics programs in the United States, but I would serve as department chair for twelve years. I also co-authored a textbook, *From Fright to Might*, now in its seventh edition. All of the royalties from book sales go to support the speech team. I created, produced, and directed a scholarship show at Mt. San Antonio called *Puttin' on the Hits* in which professors, staff, administrators, trustees, and students perform lip sync impersonations of the greatest entertainers. That annual show is still running and has raised hundreds of thousands of dollars for student scholarships.

Starting as the local president of the Community College Faculty Association, I became successively the state-wide union treasurer, vice president, and eventually the first president to serve three consecutive terms.

During these years, in addition to my teaching full-time, I began a successful real estate and mortgage company. Along the way, I owned eight pizza restaurants. Due to the malfeasance of a business partner, who raised the ire of the IRS by not paying our taxes, the business collapsed, and I ended up owing more than I owned to the federal government. I had to file for bankruptcy. Eventually all my debts were satisfied.

In 2013 I retired from teaching and became a full-time resident of Brookings, Oregon, where I began again to sell real estate. I worked for Century 21 Agate Realty for one year and then went out on my own with Pacific Ocean Properties in Brookings and eventually Reel Properties in Crescent City, California. I also own two real estate property management companies, caring for one hundred rental properties along the Pacific coast. I have spent the last seven years working very hard and God has blessed me with financial success.

In the next installment, *Overcoming All Odds: Three,* the reader will be introduced to some amazing students, who had their own challenges and demons, and who sought to better their lives with my help and the assistance of teachers who cared about them. Together we had to fight against school administrators, who were unconcerned with them as individuals needing help. I will also recount the personal problems that I was able to overcome with the help of a new set of friends who were available when I needed them most.

I hope my writings have inspired you to overcome your own difficulties and to have greater empathy for those who are working hard to surmount theirs.